Good Food Made Simple

PASTA

Good Food Made Simple

PASTA

Over 140 delicious recipes, 500 colour photographs,
step-by-step images and nutritional information

This edition published by Parragon Books Ltd in 2014
LOVE FOOD is an imprint of Parragon Books Ltd

Parragon Books Ltd
Chartist House
15–17 Trim Street
Bath BA1 1HA, UK
www.parragon.com/lovefood

ISBN 978-1-4723-5701-4

Printed in China

Additional design by Geoff Borin
New photography by Clive Bozzard-Hill
New home economy by Valerie Barrett, Carol Tennat, Sally Mansfield and Mitzie
Wilson
New recipes and introduction by Linda Doeser
Edited by Fiona Biggs
Nutritional analysis by Fiona Hunter

Notes for the Reader
This book uses both metric and imperial measurements. Follow the same
units of measurement throughout; do not mix metric and imperial. All spoon
measurements are level: teaspoons are assumed to be 5 ml, and tablespoons
are assumed to be 15 ml. Unless otherwise stated, milk is assumed to be full fat,
eggs and individual vegetables are medium, and pepper is freshly ground black
pepper. Unless otherwise stated, all root vegetables should be peeled prior to
using.

Garnishes, decorations and serving suggestions are all optional and not
necessarily included in the recipe ingredients or method. Any optional
ingredients and seasoning to taste are not included in the nutritional analysis. The
times given are an approximate guide only. Preparation times differ according
to the techniques used by different people and the cooking times may also vary
from those given. Optional ingredients, variations or serving suggestions have not
been included in the time calculations.

Contents

Perfect pasta

Pasta's immense popularity is hardly surprising, given that it is astonishingly versatile, easy to cook, nourishing, inexpensive and, in its dried form, keeps for ages. In short, it is arguably the most useful ingredient in the kitchen.

It goes with just about every other foodstuff imaginable to create a range of taste sensations – rich and creamy, light and refreshing, hot and spicy, simple and basic or luxurious and impressive. It may be served hot as a main course or cold as a substantial salad or as part of a picnic, buffet or barbecue and is a delicious and valuable addition to all kinds of soups. It is as tasty partnered with vegetarian ingredients, from tomatoes and mushrooms to cheese and herbs, as it is with all kinds of meat and poultry, fish and seafood.

Pasta is the perfect choice for today's busy lifestyle as there are many dishes that can be prepared and cooked within 30 minutes and some that take only half that time. It's great for midweek family meals, especially as almost all children really love it, and is also ideal for easy, informal entertaining. Whether you're looking for a warming and filling supper to serve on a chilly winter's evening or a delicately flavoured al fresco summer lunch, pasta fits the bill.

Nutritionists recommend that cereals should comprise 33 per cent of a well-balanced diet. Pasta is high in complex carbohydrates, providing a steady release of energy, as well as being an important source of fibre. It contains very little fat. Depending on the type of pasta, it can be a useful source of protein as well as important minerals and vitamins.

Whether you're looking for a warming and filling supper to serve on a chilly winter's evening or a delicately flavoured al fresco summer lunch, pasta fits the bill.

Pasta is very versatile so it's easy to find fabulous recipes for all occasions and every season of the year.

Types of pasta

Pasta dough is made by kneading durum wheat flour with water and sometimes eggs and flavourings, such as vegetable purées, which may also colour it. The dough is then rolled, stamped, punched or extruded to produce a vast range of different shapes. Afterwards it may be dried or sold fresh. Fresh pasta should be used within a few days of purchase; check the 'use-by' date on the packet.

Unfilled pasta

Usually dried, this pasta is boiled and then served with a sauce. It is probably the most commonly used and there are hundreds of shapes. There are no strict rules about which shape to serve with which sauce, although some are traditional partners, such as fettuccine with alfredo sauce and spaghetti with carbonara sauce. It is interesting that although spaghetti bolognese is one of the most popular dishes outside Italy, in its home country tagliatelle is the classic choice.

While it's very much a matter of personal preference, there are a few useful guidelines. Long thin pasta tubes, such as spaghetti and linguine, suit seafood and light, creamy sauces. Thicker, rich sauces go well with flat ribbons, such as tagliatelle. Smaller shapes are best with thick, chunky sauces which are easily trapped in the hollows and ridges of shells (conchiglie) and quills (penne), for example.

Pasta for filling and baking

Available both fresh and dried, this group includes lasagne – flat sheets or squares for layering with a filling – cannelloni and manicotti – wide tubes and giant shells. In the past all pasta for stuffing had to be boiled first, but modern no-precook pasta can be filled or layered and baked straightaway with plenty of sauce. Check the packet label when buying.

Filled pasta

A wide range of both fresh and dried filled pasta is available, the best known being ravioli and tortellini. Among the most popular fillings are spinach and ricotta, chicken, pork, prosciutto and pumpkin, but increasingly exotic combinations of vegetables, meat and herbs are available in supermarkets and Italian delicatessens. Although making filled pasta at home isn't especially difficult, it is very time-consuming and, even in Italy, is far less prevalent than it once was.

The most common pasta colourings come from spinach and tomato purées respectively.

Soup pasta

Tiny shapes, such as stars and rings, may be added to soups shortly before the end of the cooking time to add substance and for their attractive appearance. Sometimes fine long pasta, such as vermicelli and angel hair pasta is added. Ravioli and other filled pastas are occasionally served in a broth or clear soup.

Coloured and flavoured pasta

Both fresh and dried pasta may be coloured, most commonly green and red, made with spinach and tomato purées respectively. A combination of plain (white), red and green pasta – tricolore – is popular, perhaps because these are the colours of the Italian flag.

Other colourings and flavourings include beetroot, herbs, mushrooms, saffron and squid ink.

Wholewheat pasta

Usually sold dried, this is widely available and extremely nutritious but is usually slightly chewier than standard pasta.

Cooking pasta

Whether fresh or dried, pasta is cooked until it is al dente, that is tender but still firm to the bite. The way to test if it is ready is to remove a small piece from the pan and bite it between your front teeth, taking care not to burn your mouth. If it still feels crunchy or just too firm for your taste, it's not ready; if the texture feels right to you, then it is ready.

While cooking pasta is easy, lots of people still have problems with it sticking together. This is why some add a tablespoon of olive oil to the cooking water, but this is not, in fact, necessary if you follow a few simple rules.

• Pasta needs lots of room and lots of water. Use a large saucepan and allow 4 litres/7 pints of water for 300–450 g/10½ oz–1 lb fresh or dried pasta.

• Salt is part of the secret of preventing the pasta from sticking. Add 3 tablespoons of salt to the above quantity of water. This may sound like a huge amount in these health-conscious days but as it's dissolved in the water, you won't actually be consuming it.

• Bring the salted water to a rolling boil before adding the pasta. Shapes, such as spirals, and nests, such as tagliatelle, can simply be dropped in. Spaghetti and linguine need to be lowered in gently, curling them around the pan as they soften. Do not cover the saucepan.

• Bring the water back to a rolling boil before you start counting the cooking time. Follow the below times as a guideline:

– dried unfilled pasta 8–10 minutes

– fresh unfilled pasta 2–3 minutes

– dried filled pasta 15–20 minutes

– fresh filled pasta 8–10 minutes

Pasta is high in complex carbohydrates and provides a steady release of energy but contains hardly any fat. It can also be a good source of protein, B vitamins, potassium and iron.

- Always check the packet instructions as some fine pasta will cook more quickly.

- Start testing for doneness a couple of minutes before the cooking time is up to avoid a soggy disappointment.

- When the pasta is ready, either tip it into a colander to drain or remove from the pan with a pasta scoop, slotted spoon or kitchen tongs, depending on the type. Drain off the water but don't overdo it, as you neither need nor want the pasta to be bone dry.

- Don't leave the cooked pasta hanging around for any length of time if you can avoid it. If it does need to stand while you finish cooking the sauce, toss with a drizzle of olive oil or a knob of butter.

- When the sauce is ready, either tip the pasta into the pan or add the sauce to the pasta in a warm serving dish. Toss well with two forks to ensure that it is well mixed and the pasta is coated in the sauce. Garnish, if you like, and serve immediately.

Pasta needs a lot of room and a lot of water – salt is also part of the secret of preventing the pasta from sticking.

Common pasta sauce ingredients

Capers

These small, green flower buds of a Mediterranean shrub are sold pickled in vinegar or brine or preserved in salt. They should be rinsed before use.

Cheese

Many, but by no means all pasta dishes, are served sprinkled with grated Parmesan cheese, also known as Parmigiano Reggiano. This hard cheese has a rich, mellow and slightly salty flavour and is a lovely straw colour. It is much better to buy a block of Parmesan and grate it freshly when needed than to use tubs of ready-grated cheese which quickly lose both flavour and texture. Pecorino is a similar hard cheese from further south in Italy but is made from sheep's milk. Other cheeses feature in sauces and fillings, particularly Gorgonzola, provolone, Gruyère and ricotta.

Chillies

Fiery fresh and dried chillies are typical of southern Italian cooking. Be careful when handling fresh chillies, avoid touching sensitive skin such as your lips or around your eyes and always wash your hands thoroughly afterwards. The heat of chillies is mainly in the membranes which surround the seeds. Scraping out the seeds will remove the membranes at the same time. However, if you like hot and spicy food, you may prefer not to.

Dried mushrooms

You can buy packs of mixed mushrooms or a single variety, such as porcini (also known as ceps). Although they might seem very expensive, you need only a small quantity because the flavour is intense. They need rehydrating before you use them. Put them into a heatproof bowl, pour in hot water to cover and leave to soak for 15–30 minutes, until softened. Drain and squeeze out any excess liquid. The soaking water may be used to add extra flavour to a sauce but it is a good idea to strain it through a fine nylon strainer or a coffee filter paper first.

Garlic

Sometimes cloves are sliced or chopped and cooked with the onion in the first stage of a sauce recipe. In others, whole cloves are heated with the oil and then removed when they begin to colour. This imparts a very mild garlic flavour to the oil and to the ingredients subsequently cooked in it.

When the sauce is ready, either tip the pasta into the pan or add the sauce to the pasta in a warm serving dish.

Herbs

As a general rule, fresh herbs have a better flavour than dried ones and some herbs, such as parsley and basil, simply cannot be dried successfully. The most commonly used are bay leaves for flavouring meat sauces, parsley, a good all-rounder, basil, especially in tomato-based sauces, sage, with meat sauces and strongly flavoured cheeses, and oregano or its close relative marjoram. Oregano is often used dried. If using dried herbs, buy them in small quantities as they lose their flavour and aroma within about three months and store in a cool, dark place.

Olive oil

Virgin olive oil is best for preparing pasta sauces; reserve the expensive extra-virgin for salad dressings. The flavour varies depending on the region where it was produced. So too does the colour; it is not an indication of quality. If cost is an issue – and olive oil is quite expensive – you can use a bland cooking oil, such as sunflower.

Onions

Most recipes use standard brown onions but if you want a milder flavour and an attractive colour, you could use red or purple ones. Spanish onions, which are usually quite large, have a sweet flavour.

Passata

Sold in bottles and cartons, this is pulped tomato that has been strained to remove the seeds. It keeps well until it has been opened, after which it should be stored in the refrigerator and used within a day or two. It is useful as a basis for a variety of sauces.

Pesto

This useful and delicious sauce is made from basil, Parmesan or pecorino cheese, olive oil and pine nuts or walnuts. It is easy to make yourself (see page 276). Commercial brands vary in quality but if you find a good one, it is a useful storecupboard stand-by. Some supermarkets stock fresh pesto in the chiller cabinets. Apart from the original basil pesto, it is now made with sun-dried tomatoes, red peppers, olives and artichoke hearts.

Tomatoes

Both fresh and canned tomatoes feature in many pasta recipes. Fresh tomatoes must be sun-ripened on the vine to develop their full, sweet flavour, so if in doubt, use canned ones. However, adding 1–2 tablespoons of tomato purée will intensify the flavour if fresh tomatoes are a little tasteless. Plum tomatoes tend to be less watery than round ones and cherry tomatoes are especially sweet. Chopped canned tomatoes are not only time-saving but also are usually less watery than whole ones.

Spaghetti Bolognese *18*

Meatballs in a Creamy Sauce *20*

Rare Beef Pasta Salad *22*

Minced Beef & Pasta Soup *24*

Pasta with Beef Rolls *26*

Sausage, Bean & Roast Squash Conchiglie *28*

Tagliatelle with a Rich Meat Sauce *30*

Beef Stroganoff *32*

Beef Burger Pasta *34*

Spaghetti & Corned Beef *36*

Spaghetti with Meatloaf *38*

Macaroni & Steak *40*

Spaghetti Carbonara *42*

Spaghetti with Bacon & Crispy Breadcrumbs *44*

Pasta with Bacon & Tomatoes *46*

Turos Csusza *48*

Spicy Pasta Amatriciana *50*

Saffron Linguine *52*

Penne Pasta with Sausage *54*

Spicy Sausage Salad *56*

Italian Sausage & Pasta Soup *58*

Pepperoni Pasta *60*

Rigatoni with Chorizo & Mushrooms *62*

Linguine With Lamb & Yellow Pepper Sauce *64*

Meat

Spaghetti Bolognese

 SERVES 4

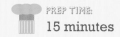 PREP TIME:
15 minutes

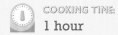 COOKING TIME:
1 hour

nutritional information per serving	535 kcals, 14g fat, 4g sat fat, 5g total sugars, 0.4g salt

This classic meat sauce (ragù) from Bologna can also be made with minced veal or half beef and half pork.

INGREDIENTS

350 g/12 oz spaghetti or pasta of your choice

fresh Parmesan cheese shavings, to garnish (optional)

sprigs of thyme, to garnish

crusty bread, to serve

bolognese sauce

2 tbsp olive oil

1 onion, finely chopped

2 garlic cloves, finely chopped

1 carrot, peeled and finely chopped

85 g/3 oz mushrooms, peeled and sliced or chopped (optional)

1 tsp dried oregano

½ tsp dried thyme

1 bay leaf

280 g/10 oz lean beef mince

300 ml/10 fl oz stock

300 ml/10 fl oz passata

salt and pepper

1. To make the sauce, heat the oil in a heavy-based, non-stick saucepan. Add the onion and sauté, half covered, for 5 minutes, or until soft. Add the garlic, carrot and mushrooms, if using, and sauté for a further 3 minutes, stirring occasionally.

2. Add the herbs and mince to the pan and cook until the meat has browned, stirring regularly.

3. Add the stock and passata. Reduce the heat, season to taste and cook over a medium–low heat, half covered, for 15–20 minutes, or until the sauce has reduced and thickened. Remove the bay leaf.

4. Meanwhile, bring a large saucepan of lightly salted water to the boil. Add the pasta, bring back to the boil and cook for 8–10 minutes, until tender but still firm to the bite. Drain well and mix together the pasta and sauce until the pasta is well coated. Serve immediately with crusty bread and garnished with Parmesan cheese shavings, if using, and sprigs of thyme.

1

2

3

Meatballs in a Creamy Sauce

 SERVES 6

 PREP TIME:
35 minutes

 COOKING TIME:
15 minutes

nutritional information per serving	690 kcals, 30g fat, 13g saturated fat, 5g sugar, 0.6g salt

This delicious regional speciality comes from the American Midwest state of Minnesota with its twin cities of Minneapolis and St. Paul.

INGREDIENTS

40 g/1½ oz fresh breadcrumbs
175 ml/6 fl oz milk
1 small onion, chopped
1 garlic clove, chopped
350 g/12 oz fresh beef mince
225 g/8 oz fresh pork mince
115 g/4 oz fresh veal mince
55 g/2 oz mashed potato
55 g/2 oz freshly grated Parmesan cheese
½ tsp ground allspice
1 tbsp chopped fresh flat-leaf parsley, plus extra to garnish
1 tbsp chopped sage
1 egg
5 tbsp plain flour
400 g/14 oz dried spaghetti
2 tbsp olive oil
175 ml/6 fl oz single cream
salt and pepper

1. Put the breadcrumbs into a small bowl, add the milk and leave to soak. Put the onion and garlic into a food processor and process to a purée. Scrape into a large bowl and add the beef, pork, veal, potato, cheese, allspice, parsley, sage and egg. Drain the breadcrumbs and add to the bowl. Season with salt and pepper and mix well.

2. Shape the mixture into balls about 2.5 cm/1 inch in diameter by rolling the mixture between the palms of your hands. Put 4 tablespoons of the flour in a shallow dish and roll the meatballs in it to coat.

3. Bring a large saucepan of lightly salted water to the boil. Add the pasta, bring back to the boil and cook for 8–10 minutes, until tender but still firm to the bite.

4. Meanwhile, heat the oil in a frying pan, add the meatballs and cook over a medium heat, shaking the pan occasionally, for 10 minutes, until evenly browned and cooked through. Remove with a slotted spoon and keep warm.

5. Stir the remaining flour into the cooking juices in the pan. Add the cream and whisk for 3–4 minutes, but do not allow the mixture to boil. Season to taste with salt and pepper and remove from the heat.

6. Drain the pasta and divide between six plates, then top with the meatballs. Spoon the sauce over and serve immediately.

Rare Beef Pasta Salad

 SERVES 4    PREP TIME:
15 minutes   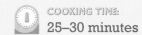 COOKING TIME:
25–30 minutes

nutritional information per serving	671 kcals, 18g fat, 4g saturated fat, 10g sugar, 1.6g salt

Thai fish sauce, also known as nam pla, is made from salted anchovies and has quite a strong flavour, so it should be used with discretion. It is available from some supermarkets and from Oriental food stores.

INGREDIENTS

450 g/1 lb rump or sirloin steak
in 1 piece
450 g/1 lb dried fusilli
4 tbsp olive oil
2 tbsp lime juice
2 tbsp Thai fish sauce
2 tsp clear honey
4 spring onions, sliced
1 cucumber, peeled and cut into
2.5-cm/1-inch chunks
3 tomatoes, cut into wedges
3 tsp finely chopped fresh mint
salt and pepper

1. Season the steak to taste with salt and pepper, then grill or pan-fry for 4 minutes on each side. Leave to rest for 5 minutes, then, using a sharp knife, slice the steak thinly across the grain and reserve until required.

2. Meanwhile, bring a large saucepan of lightly salted water to the boil. Add the pasta, bring back to the boil and cook for 8–10 minutes, until tender but still firm to the bite. Drain thoroughly and toss in the oil.

3. Mix together the lime juice, fish sauce and honey in a small saucepan and cook over a medium heat for about 2 minutes.

4. Add the spring onions, cucumber, tomato wedges and mint to the pan, then add the steak and mix well. Season to taste with salt.

5. Transfer the pasta to a large warmed serving dish and top with the steak mixture. Serve just warm or leave to cool completely.

Minced Beef & Pasta Soup

 SERVES 4    PREP TIME: 20 minutes    COOKING TIME: 35 minutes

nutritional information per serving	686 kcals, 40g fat, 19g sat fat, 5g total sugars, 1.9g salt

Quick and easy to make, this tasty soup, served with some crusty bread, is perfect for a filling lunch.

INGREDIENTS

55 g/2 oz butter

2 tbsp olive oil

1 Spanish onion, finely chopped

1 garlic clove, finely chopped

450 g/1 lb fresh beef mince

1 tsp dried oregano

3 courgettes, thinly sliced

1.7 litres/3 pints beef stock

200 g/7 oz canned tomatoes, drained and coarsely chopped

115 g/4 oz dried soup pasta, such as stars or shells

55 g/2 oz freshly grated Parmesan cheese

salt and pepper

1. Melt the butter with the oil in a large saucepan over a medium heat. Add the onion and garlic and cook, stirring occasionally, for 8 minutes, until lightly browned. Add the beef and cook, breaking it up with a wooden spoon, for 8–10 minutes, until brown.

2. Sprinkle in the oregano, add the courgettes, pour in the stock and season to taste with salt and pepper. Bring to the boil, then reduce the heat and simmer for 15 minutes.

3. Stir in the tomatoes and pasta and simmer for 5–8 minutes, until the pasta is tender. Remove from the heat and taste and adjust the seasoning, if necessary, then pour into a warmed tureen. Sprinkle with the cheese and serve immediately.

Pasta with Beef Rolls

 SERVES 4

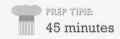 PREP TIME:
45 minutes

 COOKING TIME:
25–30 minutes

nutritional information per serving	759 kcals, 25g fat, 7.5g sat fat, 10g total sugars, 1.2g salt

This dish originates from Puglia, the region that occupies the 'heel' of Italy's 'boot', and that boasts more types of pasta than any other.

INGREDIENTS

2 garlic cloves

4 x 150-g/5½-oz very thin slices of lean beef

8 celery leaves

55 g/2 oz freshly grated Parmesan cheese

2 tsp capers, rinsed

4 tbsp olive oil

55 g/2 oz pancetta, diced

1 kg/2 lb 4 oz ripe plum tomatoes, peeled and chopped

400 g/14 oz dried orecchiette pasta

salt and pepper

1. Finely chop 1 garlic clove and peel the other. Spread out the slices of beef on a work surface and season to taste with salt and pepper. Place two celery leaves in the centre of each and scatter over the chopped garlic. Sprinkle with ½ teaspoon of the cheese and divide the capers between the beef slices. Roll up each slice like a Swiss roll and secure with a wooden cocktail stick.

2. Heat the oil with the remaining garlic in a saucepan. When it begins to colour, remove and discard the garlic. Add the pancetta to the pan and cook over a medium heat, stirring frequently, for 2–3 minutes. Reduce the heat to low, add the beef rolls and cook, turning occasionally, for 8–10 minutes, until evenly browned. Add the tomatoes, season to taste with salt and pepper and simmer, stirring occasionally, for 25–30 minutes, until the sauce has thickened.

3. Meanwhile, bring a large saucepan of lightly salted water to the boil. Add the pasta, bring back to the boil and cook for 8–10 minutes, until tender but still firm to the bite. Drain thoroughly.

4. Remove the beef rolls from the sauce and add the pasta. Toss together with two forks, then divide between four plates. Top each with a beef roll, sprinkle with the remaining cheese and serve immediately.

1

1

2

Sausage, Bean & Roast Squash Conchiglie

 SERVES 4

 PREP TIME:
25 minutes

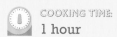 COOKING TIME:
1 hour

nutritional information per serving	695 kcals, 21g fat, 5g saturated fat, 21g sugar, 1.9g salt

This colourful and satisfying dish is full of wonderfully contrasting and complementary flavours.

INGREDIENTS

1.25 kg/2 lb 12 oz butternut squash, peeled, deseeded and cut into 2.5-cm/1-inch chunks

3 tbsp olive oil

1 onion, finely chopped

1 celery stick, finely chopped

225 g/8 oz pork sausages with herbs, skins removed

200 ml/7 fl oz red wine

250 ml/9 fl oz vegetable or chicken stock

3 tbsp sun-dried tomato paste

400 g/14 oz canned borlotti beans, drained and rinsed

280 g/10 oz dried conchiglie

4 tbsp chopped fresh flat-leaf parsley

salt and pepper

freshly grated pecorino cheese, to serve

1. Preheat the oven to 200°C/400°F/Gas Mark 6. Place the squash in a roasting tin, large enough to fit the squash in a single layer. Drizzle over 2 tablespoons of the olive oil. Toss together and roast for 25–30 minutes until tender.

2. Heat the remaining oil in a large frying pan. Add the onion and celery. Fry gently for 2 minutes until the onion turns translucent. Turn up the heat and add the sausage. Fry for another 2–3 minutes until lightly browned, breaking the sausage into small pieces as you stir.

3. Add the wine to the pan and boil rapidly until most of it has evaporated. Add the stock, sun-dried tomato paste and beans. Simmer for 10–12 minutes until the liquid has reduced and is slightly thickened.

4. Bring a large saucepan of lightly salted water to the boil. Add the pasta, bring back to the boil and cook for 8–10 minutes, until tender but still firm to the bite. Drain thoroughly and transfer to a warmed serving bowl. Add the roast squash, sausage sauce and parsley, and season to taste with salt and pepper. Serve immediately with the pecorino cheese.

Tagliatelle with a Rich Meat Sauce

 SERVES 4

 PREP TIME:
20 minutes

 COOKING TIME:
1 hour

nutritional information per serving	390 kcals, 15g fat, 4g saturated fat, 3.5g sugar, 0.7g salt

One of the world's best-known and most-loved pasta dishes, this meat sauce is classically served not with spaghetti, but with tagliatelle.

INGREDIENTS

4 tbsp olive oil, plus extra for drizzling

85 g/3 oz pancetta or streaky bacon, diced

1 onion, chopped

1 garlic clove, finely chopped

1 carrot, chopped

1 celery stick, chopped

225 g/8 oz fresh beef mince

115 g/4 oz chicken livers, chopped

2 tbsp passata

125 ml/4 fl oz dry white wine

225 ml/8 fl oz beef stock

1 tbsp chopped fresh oregano

1 bay leaf

450 g/1 lb dried tagliatelle

salt and pepper

grated Parmesan cheese, to serve

1. Heat the oil in a large heavy-based saucepan. Add the pancetta and cook over a medium heat, stirring occasionally, for 3–5 minutes, until it is just turning brown. Add the onion, garlic, carrot and celery and cook, stirring occasionally, for a further 5 minutes.

2. Add the beef and cook over a high heat, breaking up the meat with a wooden spoon, for 5 minutes, until browned. Stir in the chicken livers and cook, stirring occasionally, for a further 2–3 minutes.

3. Add the passata, wine, stock, oregano and bay leaf and season to taste with salt and pepper. Bring to the boil, reduce the heat, cover and simmer for 30–35 minutes.

4. Meanwhile, bring a large saucepan of lightly salted water to the boil. Add the pasta, bring back to the boil and cook for 8–10 minutes, until tender but still firm to the bite.

5. Drain the pasta and transfer to a warmed serving dish. Drizzle with a little oil and toss well. Remove and discard the bay leaf from the sauce, then pour the sauce over the pasta and toss again. Serve immediately with the Parmesan cheese for sprinkling over.

1

2

3

Beef Stroganoff

 SERVES 4

 PREP TIME:
10 minutes
plus soaking

 COOKING TIME:
10–15 minutes

nutritional information per serving	631 kcals, 23g fat, 10g sat fat, 4g total sugars, 0.2g salt

Beef stroganoff gets its name from the 19th century Russian diplomat Count Paul Stroganov. The delicious creamy sauce and the combination of red wine and garlic give it an unforgettable flavour.

INGREDIENTS

15 g/½ oz dried porcini
350 g/12 oz beef fillet
2 tbsp olive oil
115 g/4 oz shallots, sliced
175 g/6 oz chestnut mushrooms
400 g/14 oz pappardelle
½ tsp Dijon mustard
5 tbsp double cream
salt and pepper
fresh chives, to garnish

1. Place the dried porcini in a bowl and cover with hot water. Leave to soak for 20 minutes. Meanwhile, cut the beef against the grain into 5-mm/¼-inch thick slices, then into 1-cm/½-inch long strips, and reserve.

2. Drain the porcini, reserving the soaking liquid, and chop. Strain the soaking liquid through a fine-mesh sieve or coffee filter and reserve.

3. Heat half the oil in a large frying pan. Add the shallots and cook over a low heat, stirring occasionally, for 5 minutes, or until softened. Add the soaked porcini, reserved soaking water and whole chestnut mushrooms to the frying pan and cook, stirring frequently, for 10 minutes, or until almost all of the liquid has evaporated. Transfer the mixture to a plate.

4. Meanwhile, bring a large saucepan of lightly salted water to the boil. Add the pasta, bring back to the boil and cook for 8–10 minutes, until tender but still firm to the bite.

5. Heat the remaining oil in the frying pan, add the beef and cook, stirring frequently, for 4 minutes, or until browned all over. You may need to do this in batches. Return the mushroom mixture to the pan and season to taste with salt and pepper. Place the mustard and cream in a small bowl and stir to mix, then fold into the meat and mushroom mixture. Heat through gently, then serve immediately with the freshly cooked pasta, garnished with chives.

Beef Burger Pasta

 SERVES 4

 PREP TIME: 10 minutes

 COOKING TIME: 15 minutes

nutritional information **per serving** : 686 kcals, 34g fat, 12g saturated fat, 8g sugar, 0.9g salt

This is a good way to use up leftover burgers, combining them with larder ingredients for a quick and easy meal.

INGREDIENTS

300 g/10½ oz dried conchiglie

350 g/12 oz beef burgers

400 g/14 oz frozen mixed vegetables, such as broccoli, carrots and sweetcorn

400 g/14 oz canned tomatoes, drained

1 garlic clove, finely chopped

1–1½ pickled jalapeño chillies, finely chopped

3 tbsp olive oil

2 tbsp freshly grated Parmesan cheese

salt and pepper

1. Preheat the grill. Meanwhile, bring a large saucepan of lightly salted water to the boil. Add the pasta, bring back to the boil and cook for 8–10 minutes, until tender but still firm to the bite.

2. Cook the burgers under the preheated grill for 7–8 minutes on each side until cooked through. Meanwhile, bring a separate saucepan of lightly salted water to the boil, add the frozen vegetables and cook for about 5 minutes.

3. Drain the vegetables, transfer to a food processor and process briefly until chopped, then tip into a saucepan. Transfer the cooked burgers to the food processor and process briefly until chopped, then add to the pan of vegetables. Stir in the tomatoes, garlic, chillies and oil, season to taste with salt and pepper and reheat gently.

4. Drain the pasta and tip it into a warmed serving bowl. Add the burger and vegetable mixture and toss lightly. Sprinkle with the cheese and serve immediately.

SOMETHING
DIFFERENT
If serving to young
children or if you
just don't like spicy
food, omit the chillies
and add a pinch of
dried oregano instead.

Spaghetti & Corned Beef

 SERVES 4

 PREP TIME:
15 minutes

 COOKING TIME:
25–30 minutes

nutritional information
per serving | 742 kcals, 21g fat, 8g saturated fat, 8g sugar, 2.8g salt

*Popular with children and extremely economical, this
variation of corned beef hash is an easy way to
ring the changes in the family menu.*

INGREDIENTS

2 tbsp sunflower oil

1 large onion, chopped

2–3 garlic cloves, finely chopped

500 g/1 lb 2 oz corned beef, chopped

400 g/14 oz canned tomatoes

450 g/1 lb dried spaghetti

2 tbsp chopped fresh parsley

pinch of crushed chillies or dash of Tabasco sauce or Worcestershire sauce

salt and pepper

1. Heat the oil in a large frying pan, add the onion and garlic and cook over a medium heat for 5 minutes until just beginning to colour.

2. Add the corned beef and cook, stirring and mashing with a wooden spoon, for 5–8 minutes until it is quite dry. Drain the tomatoes, reserving the can juices, and stir them into the pan. Cook for a further 10 minutes, adding a little of the reserved can juices if the mixture seems to be drying out too much.

3. Meanwhile, bring a large saucepan of lightly salted water to the boil. Add the pasta, bring back to the boil and cook for 8–10 minutes, until tender but still firm to the bite.

4. Drain the pasta and add it to the frying pan. Stir in the parsley and chillies and season to taste with salt and pepper, bearing in mind that corned beef is often quite salty already. Mix well and heat through for a further few minutes. Serve immediately.

HEALTHY HINT
You can buy cans of reduced-salt corned beef if you are concerned about the levels of salt in your diet.

Spaghetti with Meatloaf

 SERVES 4

 PREP TIME: 10 minutes

 COOKING TIME: 25 minutes

nutritional information
per serving   719 kcals, 19g fat, 7g sat fat, 10g total sugars, 0.9g salt

While freshly cooked meatloaf is delicious, cold leftovers are a bit dull, so why not use them up in this tasty pasta dish?

INGREDIENTS

2 tbsp olive oil

1 onion, chopped

1 garlic clove, finely chopped

400 g/14 oz meatloaf

3 tbsp brandy

400 g/14 oz canned chopped tomatoes

450 g/1 lb dried spaghetti

150 g/5½ oz frozen mixed vegetables

1 tbsp chopped fresh flat-leaf parsley

salt and pepper

freshly grated Parmesan cheese, to serve

1. Heat the oil in a saucepan, add the onion and garlic and cook over a low heat, stirring occasionally, for 5 minutes until soft.

2. Crumble the meatloaf into the pan and cook, stirring frequently, for a few minutes. Meanwhile, bring a large saucepan of lightly salted water to the boil.

3. Add the brandy to the pan with the meatloaf, increase the heat to medium and cook for 5 minutes. Stir in the tomatoes. Bring to the boil, reduce the heat and simmer, stirring occasionally, for 10 minutes.

4. Meanwhile, add the pasta to the pan of boiling water, bring back to the boil and cook for 5 minutes. Add the frozen vegetables, bring back to the boil and cook for a further 5 minutes, until the pasta is tender but still firm to the bite. Drain the pasta and vegetables, add to the pan with the sauce and toss to coat. Season to taste with salt and pepper, sprinkle with the parsley and serve immediately, handing the Parmesan cheese separately.

SOMETHING
DIFFERENT
If you prefer
you could substitute
red wine or chicken
stock for the
brandy in step 3.

Macaroni & Steak

SERVES 4–6

PREP TIME:
15 minutes

COOKING TIME:
1 hour

nutritional information
per serving

355 kcals, 17g fat, 7.5g saturated fat, 7g sugar, 0.8g salt

This is a terrific dish for easy entertaining, especially as you can have it all ready to go in the oven before your guests arrive.

INGREDIENTS

2 tbsp olive oil

1 onion, chopped

2 garlic cloves, finely chopped

450 g/1 lb rump steak, cut into thin strips

2 tbsp tomato purée

1 tbsp plain flour

1 tbsp sweet paprika

300 ml/10 fl oz hot beef stock

115 g/4 oz dried elbow macaroni

2 beef tomatoes, sliced

450 g/1 lb Greek-style yogurt

2 eggs, lightly beaten

salt and pepper

1. Heat the oil in a large saucepan, add the onion and garlic and cook over a low heat, stirring occasionally, for 5 minutes. Add the steak, increase the heat to medium, and cook, stirring frequently, for 2–3 minutes, or until evenly browned.

2. Stir in the tomato purée, sprinkle in the flour and paprika and cook, stirring, for 1 minute. Stir in the stock, season to taste with salt and pepper and bring to the boil. Reduce the heat and simmer for 10 minutes.

3. Meanwhile, preheat the oven to 190°C/375°F/Gas Mark 5. Bring a saucepan of lightly salted water to the boil. Add the pasta, bring back to the boil and cook for 8–10 minutes, until tender but still firm to the bite.

4. Spoon the steak mixture into an ovenproof dish and cover with the tomato slices. Drain the pasta, tip it into a bowl and stir in the yogurt and eggs. Spoon the pasta on top of the tomatoes and bake in the preheated oven for 30 minutes. Remove from the oven and serve immediately.

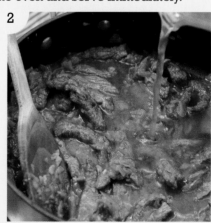

GOES WELL WITH
This substantial
dish requires
nothing more than
a mixed leaf
salad with some
herbs and a light
dressing.

Spaghetti Carbonara

 SERVES 4    PREP TIME: 15 minutes    COOKING TIME: 25–30 minutes

nutritional information per serving	1498 kcals, 73g fat, 35g sat fat, 7g total sugars, 4g salt

This popular Italian dish combines pancetta and double cream with two hard cheeses – Parmesan and pecorino.

INGREDIENTS

400 g/14 oz dried spaghetti

4 eggs

4 tbsp double cream

55 g/2 oz grated Parmesan cheese, plus extra to garnish

55 g/2 oz grated pecorino cheese

1 tbsp butter

150 g/5½ oz pancetta, finely diced

salt and pepper

1. Bring a large saucepan of lightly salted water to the boil. Add the pasta, bring back to the boil and cook for 8–10 minutes, until tender but still firm to the bite.

2. Meanwhile, stir together the eggs, cream, Parmesan cheese and pecorino cheese in a bowl. Season to taste with salt and pepper.

3. Melt the butter in a large saucepan, add the pancetta, and fry over a medium heat for 8-10 minutes, until crispy. Drain the spaghetti and add it to the pan while still dripping wet. Pour the cheese sauce over it. Remove the pan from the heat. Toss the spaghetti in the sauce until the eggs begin to thicken but are still creamy.

4. Transfer to warmed plates and serve immediately, sprinkled with pepper and a little more Parmesan cheese.

COOK'S NOTE
For a more substantial dish, cook one to two finely chopped shallots with the pancetta and add 115 g/4 oz sliced mushrooms.

Spaghetti with Bacon
& Crispy Breadcrumbs

 SERVES 2    PREP TIME: 10 minutes    COOKING TIME: 20 minutes

nutritional information per serving	787 kcals, 42g fat, 11g sat fat, 4g total sugars, 2.7g salt

Quick, easy and economical, yet truly mouth-watering, this is the perfect midweek family supper.

INGREDIENTS

55 g/2 oz day-old ciabatta bread (approximately one roll)

sprig of fresh rosemary

175 g/6 oz dried spaghetti

2 tsp olive oil

140 g/5 oz smoked streaky bacon, chopped

15 g/½ oz butter

40 g/1½ oz pine kernels

2 garlic cloves, crushed

2–3 tbsp chopped fresh flat-leaf parsley

salt and pepper

1. Put the day-old bread, including any crusts, in a food processor or blender and process until the mixture resembles coarse breadcrumbs. Bruise the rosemary sprig in a pestle and mortar or using a rolling pin to release the flavour.

2. Bring a large saucepan of lightly salted water to the boil. Add the pasta, bring back to the boil and cook for 8–10 minutes, until tender but still firm to the bite.

3. Meanwhile, heat the oil in a large frying pan, add the bacon and rosemary and fry for 2–3 minutes until the bacon is golden brown. Transfer to a warmed serving bowl using a slotted spoon.

4. Add the butter to the bacon fat remaining in the pan. When melted and foaming, add the breadcrumbs, pine kernels and garlic. Fry for 2–3 minutes, stirring until golden brown, then tip into the bowl with the bacon.

5. Drain the pasta and transfer to the bowl with the bacon and breadcrumbs. Add the parsley, season with pepper and toss well. Serve immediately.

Pasta with Bacon & Tomatoes

 SERVES 4    PREP TIME: 10 minutes    COOKING TIME: 35–40 minutes

nutritional information **per serving** — 592 kcals, 17g fat, 8g sat fat, 10g total sugars, 1.5g salt

This is an ideal dish to serve in the summer when tomatoes are at their sweetest.

INGREDIENTS

900 g/2 lb small, sweet tomatoes

6 rashers rindless smoked bacon

55 g/2 oz butter

1 onion, chopped

1 garlic clove, crushed

4 fresh oregano sprigs, finely chopped

450 g/1 lb dried orecchiette

salt and pepper

freshly grated pecorino cheese, to serve

1. Blanch the tomatoes in boiling water. Drain, peel and deseed the tomatoes, then roughly chop the flesh.

2. Using a sharp knife, chop the bacon into small dice. Melt the butter in a saucepan. Add the bacon and cook for 2-3 minutes until golden brown.

3. Add the onion and garlic and cook over a medium heat for 5–7 minutes, until just softened.

4. Add the tomatoes and oregano to the pan and then season to taste with salt and pepper. Lower the heat and simmer for 10–12 minutes.

5. Bring a large saucepan of lightly salted water to the boil. Add the pasta, bring back to the boil and cook for 8–10 minutes, until tender but still firm to the bite. Drain the pasta and transfer to a warmed serving bowl. Spoon the bacon and tomato sauce over the pasta, toss to coat and serve immediately with the pecorino cheese.

Turos Csusza

 SERVES 6

 PREP TIME: 10 minutes

 COOKING TIME: 15 minutes

nutritional information **per serving**   510 kcals, 21g fat, 12g sat fat, 6g total sugars, 1g salt

This is an updated version of a Hungarian dish originally consisting of home-made noodles, sheep's milk cheese, bacon and smetana (a type of soured cream).

INGREDIENTS

450 g/1 lb dried pasta spirals or elbow macaroni

4 smoked back bacon rashers

450 ml/16 fl oz soured cream

350 g/12 oz cottage cheese

salt

1. Preheat the oven to 180°C/350°F/Gas Mark 4 and preheat the grill. Bring a large saucepan of lightly salted water to the boil, add the pasta, bring back to the boil and cook for 8–10 minutes, until tender but still firm to the bite.

2. Meanwhile, cook the bacon under the preheated grill for 3–4 minutes on each side, until crisp. Remove from the heat and crumble.

3. Drain the pasta, tip it into an ovenproof dish and stir in the soured cream. Sprinkle with the cottage cheese, then with the crumbled bacon and lightly season with salt. Bake in the preheated oven for 5 minutes, then serve straight from the dish.

2

3

3

SOMETHING
DIFFERENT
For a stronger,
more authentic
flavour, substitute
crumbled feta
cheese for the
cottage cheese.

Spicy Pasta Amatriciana

 SERVES 4    PREP TIME: 25 minutes   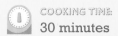 COOKING TIME: 30 minutes

nutritional information **per serving** | 694 kcals, 24g fat, 9g saturated fat, 11g sugar, 2g salt

Traditionally served with bucatini, this dish from the town of Amatrice in central Italy is served to celebrate the national August holiday.

INGREDIENTS

2 tbsp olive oil

1 large onion, finely chopped

2 garlic cloves, finely chopped

175 g/6 oz pancetta or bacon, diced

1–2 red chillies, deseeded and chopped, or ½–1 tsp crushed dried chillies

3 tbsp dry white wine

800 g/1 lb 12 oz canned chopped tomatoes

450 g/1 lb dried bucatini or spaghetti

85 g/3 oz pecorino cheese, freshly grated

salt and pepper

1. Heat the oil in a large saucepan, add the onion and garlic and cook over a low heat, stirring occasionally, for 5 minutes. Add the pancetta and chillies, increase the heat to medium and cook, stirring frequently, for 5–8 minutes, until the onion is lightly browned.

2. Pour in the wine, bring to the boil and boil rapidly for 2 minutes, then stir in the tomatoes and season to taste with salt and pepper. Bring back to the boil, then reduce the heat to low and simmer, stirring occasionally, for 15 minutes.

3. Meanwhile, bring a large saucepan of lightly salted water to the boil. Add the pasta, bring back to the boil and cook for 8–10 minutes, until tender but still firm to the bite.

4. Drain the pasta, tip into the pan with the sauce and toss to coat. Transfer to a warmed serving dish, sprinkle with half the cheese and serve immediately, with the remaining cheese on the side.

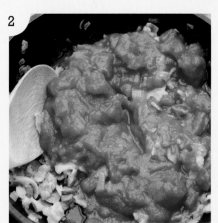

SOMETHING DIFFERENT
For additional flavour, add 1 tablespoon of chopped flat-leaf parsley, five to six torn basil leaves or a generous pinch of dried oregano to the tomatoes.

Saffron Linguine

nutritional information per serving	650 kcals, 33g fat, 19g saturated fat, 3g sugar, 1.3g salt

Saffron gives this delightful dish its delicate colour, pungently sweet aroma and unique flavour.

INGREDIENTS

350 g/12 oz dried linguine
pinch of saffron threads
2 tbsp water
140 g/5 oz cooked ham, cut into strips
175 ml/6 fl oz double cream
55 g/2 oz freshly grated Parmesan cheese
2 egg yolks
salt and pepper

1. Bring a large saucepan of lightly salted water to the boil. Add the pasta, bring back to the boil and cook for 8–10 minutes, until tender but still firm to the bite.

2. Meanwhile, place the saffron in a saucepan and add the water. Bring to the boil, then remove from the heat and leave to stand for 5 minutes.

3. Stir the ham, cream and cheese into the saffron and return the pan to the heat. Season to taste with salt and pepper and heat through gently, stirring constantly, until simmering. Remove from the heat and beat in the egg yolks. Drain the pasta and transfer to a warmed serving dish. Add the saffron sauce, toss well and serve immediately.

2

3

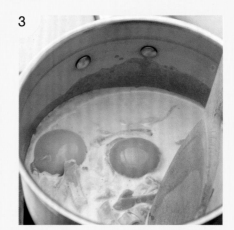
3

VARIATION
You don't have to use
cooked ham in this
dish. For a richer
flavour try using
prosciutto or parma
ham, or even bacon.

Penne Pasta with Sausage

 SERVES 4–6    PREP TIME: 15 minutes   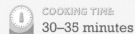 COOKING TIME: 30–35 minutes

nutritional information **per serving** | 437 kcals, 19g fat, 6g saturated fat, 5g sugar, 1.5g salt

Packed with flavour and lively rather than fiery, this is an ideal dish for informal entertaining.

INGREDIENTS

2 tbsp olive oil
1 red onion, roughly chopped
2 garlic cloves, roughly chopped
6 Italian sausages, skinned and the meat crumbled
½ tsp dried chilli flakes
2 tbsp chopped fresh oregano
400 g/14 oz canned chopped tomatoes
350 g/12 oz dried penne
salt and pepper

1. Heat the oil in a large saucepan, add the onion and cook over a medium heat, stirring frequently, for 6–8 minutes until starting to brown. Add the garlic and the crumbled sausages and cook for 8–10 minutes, breaking up the sausages with a wooden spoon.

2. Add the chilli flakes and oregano and stir well. Pour in the tomatoes and bring to the boil. Place over a low heat and simmer for 4–5 minutes until reduced and thickened. Season to taste with salt and pepper.

3. Meanwhile, bring a large saucepan of lightly salted water to the boil. Add the pasta, bring back to the boil and cook for 8–10 minutes, until tender but still firm to the bite. Drain thoroughly and return to the pan.

4. Pour the sauce into the pasta and stir well. Transfer to warmed serving plates and serve immediately.

Spicy Sausage Salad

 SERVES 4   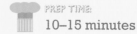 PREP TIME: 10–15 minutes    COOKING TIME: 20–25 minutes

nutritional information **per serving** | 634 kcals, 33g fat, 10g saturated fat, 12g sugar, 1.3g salt

A warm salad adds variety to the family menu and is delicious at any time of year.

INGREDIENTS

125 g/4½ oz dried conchiglie

2 tbsp olive oil

1 medium onion, chopped

2 garlic cloves, very finely chopped

1 small yellow pepper, deseeded and cut into matchsticks

175 g/6 oz spicy pork sausage, such as chorizo, Italian pepperoni or salami, skinned and sliced

2 tbsp red wine

1 tbsp red wine vinegar

125 g/4½ oz mixed salad leaves

salt

1. Bring a large saucepan of lightly salted water to the boil. Add the pasta, bring back to the boil and cook for 8–10 minutes, until tender but still firm to the bite. Drain thoroughly and reserve.

2. Heat the oil in a saucepan over a medium heat. Add the onion and cook until translucent. Stir in the garlic, yellow pepper and sausage and cook for about 3–4 minutes, stirring once or twice.

3. Add the wine, vinegar and reserved pasta to the pan, stir and bring the mixture just to the boil over a medium heat.

4. Arrange the salad leaves on warmed serving plates, spoon over the warm sausage and pasta mixture and serve immediately.

GOES WELL WITH
For contrast, serve with a sprouted seed salad incorporating some peppery leaves such as rocket or watercress and a creamy yogurt dressing.

Italian Sausage & Pasta Soup

 SERVES 4

 PREP TIME: 20 minutes

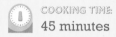 COOKING TIME: 45 minutes

nutritional information per serving	552 kcals, 27g fat, 9g sat fat, 9g total sugars, 3.5g salt

Served with some crusty bread, this filling soup makes a meal in a bowl - ideal for family lunch on busy weekends.

INGREDIENTS

2 tbsp olive oil

1 onion, chopped

1 carrot, chopped

1 celery stick, chopped

450 g/1 lb Italian sausages, skinned and crumbled

2 garlic cloves, finely chopped

2 bay leaves

½ tsp dried oregano

1 tsp crushed chillies (optional)

400 g/14 oz canned chopped tomatoes

850 ml/1½ pints chicken stock

400 g/14 oz canned cannellini beans, drained

115 g/4 oz dried soup pasta, such as conchiglie

2 tbsp chopped fresh flat-leaf parsley

salt and pepper

freshly grated Parmesan cheese, to serve

crusty bread, to serve

1. Heat the oil in a large saucepan, add the onion, carrot and celery and cook over a low heat, stirring occasionally, for 5 minutes. Stir in the crumbled sausages and garlic, increase the heat to medium and cook, stirring frequently, for a further few minutes until the meat is brown.

2. Add the bay leaves, oregano, crushed chillies, if using, tomatoes and stock and bring to the boil, stirring frequently. Reduce the heat, partially cover and simmer for 30 minutes.

3. Stir in the beans and pasta and simmer for a further 5–8 minutes, until the pasta is tender but still firm to the bite. Season to taste with salt and pepper, stir in the parsley and remove from the heat. Remove and discard the bay leaves, ladle the soup into warmed mugs or bowls and serve immediately, with the cheese separately and crusty bread.

Pepperoni Pasta

 SERVES 4    PREP TIME: 10 minutes    COOKING TIME: 20 minutes

nutritional information per serving	780 kcals, 33g fat, 10g saturated fat, 14g sugar, 2.8g salt

A sure-fire favourite, this colourful and utterly scrumptious dish will cheer up even the dreariest day.

INGREDIENTS

3 tbsp olive oil

1 onion, chopped

1 red pepper, deseeded and diced

1 orange pepper, deseeded and diced

800 g/1 lb 12 oz canned chopped tomatoes

1 tbsp sun-dried tomato paste

1 tsp paprika

225 g/8 oz pepperoni sausage, sliced

2 tbsp chopped fresh flat-leaf parsley, plus extra to garnish

450 g/1 lb dried penne

salt and pepper

1. Heat 2 tablespoons of the oil in a large heavy-based frying pan. Add the onion and cook over a low heat, stirring occasionally, for 5 minutes, or until softened. Add the red pepper and orange pepper, tomatoes and their can juices, sun-dried tomato paste and paprika and bring to the boil.

2. Add the pepperoni and parsley and season to taste with salt and pepper. Stir well, bring to the boil, then reduce the heat and simmer for 10–15 minutes.

3. Meanwhile, bring a large saucepan of lightly salted water to the boil. Add the pasta, bring back to the boil and cook for 8–10 minutes, until tender but still firm to the bite. Drain well and transfer to a warmed serving dish. Add the remaining olive oil and toss. Add the sauce and toss again. Sprinkle with parsley and serve immediately.

COOK'S NOTE

Pepperoni is a hotly spiced Italian sausage made from pork and beef and flavoured with fennel. You could substitute another spicy sausage, such as chorizo.

Rigatoni with Chorizo & Mushrooms

 SERVES 4    PREP TIME: 15 minutes    COOKING TIME: 25–30 minutes

| nutritional information per serving | 668 kcals, 29g fat, 9g saturated fat, 6g sugar, 1g salt |

This is a delightfully rustic and earthy dish – real comfort food that is also quick and easy to prepare.

INGREDIENTS

4 tbsp olive oil

1 red onion, chopped

1 garlic clove, chopped

1 celery stick, sliced

400 g/14 oz dried rigatoni

280 g/10 oz chorizo sausage, sliced

225 g/8 oz chestnut mushrooms, halved

1 tbsp chopped fresh coriander

1 tbsp lime juice

salt and pepper

1. Heat the oil in a frying pan. Add the onion, garlic and celery and cook over a low heat, stirring occasionally, for 5 minutes, until softened.

2. Meanwhile, bring a large saucepan of lightly salted water to the boil. Add the pasta, bring back to the boil and cook for 8–10 minutes, until tender but still firm to the bite.

3. While the pasta is cooking, add the chorizo to the frying pan and cook, stirring occasionally, for 5 minutes, until evenly browned. Add the mushrooms and cook, stirring occasionally, for a further 5 minutes. Stir in the coriander and lime juice and season to taste with salt and pepper.

4. Drain the pasta and return it to the pan. Add the chorizo and mushroom mixture and toss. Divide between warmed plates and serve immediately.

GOES WELL WITH
Cheese focaccia, warm ciabatta with sun-dried tomatoes or plain hot rolls will turn this dish into a feast.

Linguine with Lamb & Yellow Pepper Sauce

 SERVES 4　　 PREP TIME: 15 minutes　　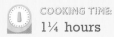 COOKING TIME: 1¼ hours

nutritional information **per serving** 485 kcals, 18g fat, 4.5g saturated fat, 9g sugar, 0.2g salt

This unusual and richly flavoured dish is a speciality from Sicily, an island where pasta features in at least one meal every day.

INGREDIENTS

4 tbsp olive oil

280 g/10 oz boneless lamb, cubed

1 garlic clove, finely chopped

1 bay leaf

125 ml/4 fl oz dry white wine

2 large yellow peppers, deseeded and diced

4 tomatoes, peeled and chopped

250 g/9 oz dried linguine

salt and pepper

1. Heat half the olive oil in a large, heavy-based frying pan. Add the lamb and cook over a medium heat, stirring frequently, until browned on all sides. Add the garlic and cook for a further minute. Add the bay leaf, pour in the wine and season to taste with salt and pepper. Bring to the boil and cook for 5 minutes, or until reduced.

2. Stir in the remaining oil, peppers and tomatoes. Reduce the heat, cover and simmer, stirring occasionally, for 45 minutes.

3. Meanwhile, bring a large saucepan of lightly salted water to the boil. Add the pasta, bring back to the boil and cook for 8–10 minutes, until tender but still firm to the bite. Drain and transfer to a warmed serving dish. Remove and discard the bay leaf from the lamb sauce and spoon the sauce over the pasta and toss. Serve immediately.

GOES WELL WITH
A simple mixed leaf
salad with a lemon
vinaigrette dressing
would be a refreshing
accompaniment to this
hearty dish.

Farfalle with Chicken & Broccoli *68*

Fettuccine with Chicken & Onion Cream Sauce *70*

Italian Chicken Soup *72*

Chicken Soup with Angel Hair Pasta *74*

Chicken, Bacon & Avocado Salad *76*

Honey & Chicken Pasta Salad *78*

Pasta & Chicken Medley *80*

Pappardelle with Chicken & Porcini Mushrooms *82*

Chicken Meatball Pasta *84*

Chicken with Creamy Penne *86*

Spaghetti with Parsley Chicken *88*

Cajun Chicken Pasta *90*

Penne with Chicken & Feta Cheese *92*

Spicy Chicken Pasta *94*

Pasta with Two Sauces *96*

Turkey & Pasta Soup *98*

Mexican Spaghetti & Meatballs *100*

Turkey Tetrazzini *102*

Giant Pasta Shells with Turkey *104*

Turkey Pasta Primavera *106*

Pasta with Chilli Barbecue Sauce *108*

Pasta with Harissa Turkey Meatballs *110*

Fettuccine with Duck Sauce *112*

Venetian Duck with Spaghetti *114*

Poultry

Farfalle with Chicken & Broccoli

 SERVES 4    PREP TIME: 15–20 minutes    COOKING TIME: 20–25 minutes

nutritional information per serving	707 kcals, 33g fat, 12g sat fat, 3g total sugars, 0.7g salt

This is one of those dishes that looks almost too pretty to eat but it's far too tasty to resist.

INGREDIENTS

4 tbsp olive oil

5 tbsp butter

3 garlic cloves, very finely chopped

450 g/1 lb skinless, boneless chicken breasts, diced

¼ tsp dried chilli flakes

450 g/1 lb small broccoli florets

300 g/10½ oz dried farfalle

175 g/6 oz bottled roasted red peppers, drained and diced

250 ml/9 fl oz chicken stock

salt and pepper

1. Bring a large saucepan of lightly salted water to the boil. Meanwhile, heat the oil and butter in a large frying pan over a medium–low heat and cook the garlic until just beginning to colour.

2. Add the diced chicken, increase the heat to medium and cook for 4–5 minutes, until the chicken is cooked through. Add the chilli flakes and season to taste with salt and pepper. Remove from the heat.

3. Plunge the broccoli into the boiling water and cook for 2 minutes. Remove with a slotted spoon and set aside. Bring the water back to the boil. Add the pasta and cook for 8–10 minutes, until tender but still firm to the bite. Drain thoroughly and add to the chicken mixture in the frying pan. Add the broccoli and roasted peppers. Pour in the stock. Simmer briskly over a medium–high heat, stirring frequently, until most of the liquid has been absorbed.

4. Transfer to warmed dishes and serve immediately.

Fettuccine with Chicken & Onion Cream Sauce

 SERVES 4

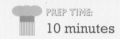 PREP TIME:
10 minutes

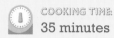 COOKING TIME:
35 minutes

nutritional information per serving	1087 kcals, 57g fat, 32g saturated fat, 8g sugar, 1.4g salt

The impressively luxurious taste belies the simplicity of this dish and the ease with which it can be prepared.

INGREDIENTS

1 tbsp olive oil

2 tbsp butter

1 garlic clove, very finely chopped

4 skinless, boneless chicken breasts

1 onion, finely chopped

1 chicken stock cube, crumbled

125 ml/4 fl oz water

300 ml/10 fl oz double cream

175 ml/6 fl oz milk

6 spring onions, green part included, sliced diagonally

35 g/1¼ oz freshly grated Parmesan cheese

450 g/1 lb dried fettuccine

salt and pepper

chopped fresh flat-leaf parsley, to garnish

1. Heat the oil and butter with the garlic in a large frying pan over a medium–low heat. Cook the garlic until just beginning to colour. Add the chicken and increase the heat to medium. Cook for 4–5 minutes on each side, until cooked through and the juices run clear. Season to taste with salt and pepper. Remove from the heat. Remove the chicken from the pan, leaving the oil in the pan. Slice the chicken diagonally into thin strips and set aside.

2. Reheat the oil in the pan. Add the onion and gently cook for 5 minutes until soft. Add the crumbled stock cube and the water. Bring to the boil, then simmer over a medium–low heat for 10 minutes. Stir in the cream, milk, spring onions and Parmesan cheese. Simmer until heated through and slightly thickened.

3. Meanwhile, bring a large saucepan of lightly salted water to the boil. Add the pasta, bring back to the boil and cook for 8–10 minutes, until tender but still firm to the bite. Drain and transfer to a warmed serving dish. Layer the chicken slices over the pasta. Pour over the sauce, garnish with parsley and serve immediately.

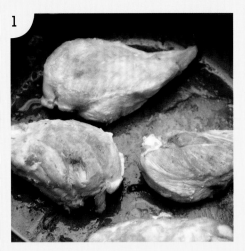

1

1

2

Italian Chicken Soup

 SERVES 4    PREP TIME: 10 minutes    COOKING TIME: 30–35 minutes

nutritional information per serving	542 kcals, 23g fat, 13g sat fat, 5.5g total sugars, 1.3g salt

A substantial soup that is full of flavour, this would make a quick and easy lunchtime meal-in-a-bowl.

INGREDIENTS

450 g/1 lb skinless, boneless chicken breasts, cut into thin strips

1.2 litres/2 pints chicken stock

150 ml/5 fl oz double cream

115 g/4 oz dried vermicelli

1 tbsp cornflour

3 tbsp milk

175 g/6 oz canned sweetcorn kernels, drained

salt and pepper

basil leaf, to garnish

1. Place the chicken in a large saucepan and pour in the chicken stock and cream. Bring to the boil, then reduce the heat and simmer for 20 minutes.

2. Meanwhile, bring a large saucepan of lightly salted water to the boil. Add the pasta, bring back to the boil and cook for 8–10 minutes, until tender but still firm to the bite. Drain thoroughly and keep warm.

3. Mix the cornflour and milk together until a smooth paste forms, then stir it into the soup. Season to taste with salt and pepper, add the sweetcorn and pasta and heat through. Ladle the soup into warmed soup bowls garnished with a basil leaf and serve immediately.

GOES WELL WITH
This is perfect
with thinly sliced,
lightly toasted bread
sprinkled with
grated Parmesan and
paprika and baked
for 10 minutes.

Chicken Soup with Angel Hair Pasta

 SERVES 6    PREP TIME: 10 minutes    COOKING TIME: 40 minutes

nutritional information **per serving**   252 kcals, 10g fat, 2g sat fat, 0.5g total sugars, 0.9g salt

This is a truly filling and nourishing soup with a delicate flavour - the perfect lunchtime pick-me-up on a dreary day.

INGREDIENTS

3 large eggs

3 tbsp water

2 tbsp chopped flat-leaf parsley

1 x 175-g/6-oz skinless boneless chicken breast

2 tbsp olive oil, plus extra for brushing

1.5 litres/2¾ pints chicken stock

115 g/4 oz dried angel hair pasta

salt and pepper

1. Preheat the grill. Lightly beat the eggs with the water and a pinch of salt in a bowl and stir in the parsley. Season the chicken with salt and pepper and brush with oil. Grill for 4–5 minutes on each side, until cooked through and the juices run clear, then remove from the heat and cut into thin strips.

2. Heat the oil in a 20-cm/8-inch omelette pan, then add a quarter of the egg mixture, swirling the pan to spread it evenly. Cook over a medium–low heat until the underside is set, then flip over with a spatula and cook for a further few seconds. Slide the omelette out of the pan and reserve. Cook three more omelettes in the same way, then roll them up and cut into thin slices to make threads.

3. Pour the stock into a large saucepan and bring to the boil. Add the pasta, breaking up the 'nests', bring back to the boil and cook for 5 minutes until tender but still firm to the bite. Add the chicken, season to taste with salt and pepper and cook for a further 3–5 minutes. Stir in the sliced omelette, remove from the heat and serve immediately.

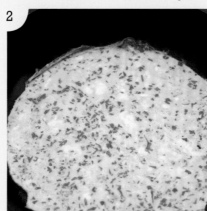

Chicken, Bacon & Avocado Salad

 SERVES 2

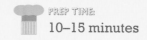 PREP TIME:
10–15 minutes

 COOKING TIME:
20 minutes

nutritional information
per serving 898 kcals, 56g fat, 10g saturated fat, 6g sugar, 1g salt

This irresistible classic partnership is given a new twist when combined with pasta and served with a vinaigrette.

INGREDIENTS

150 g/5½ oz dried farfalle

2 thick rashers smoked
streaky bacon

200 g/7 oz cooked skinless,
boneless chicken breasts, sliced

2 plum tomatoes, sliced

1 large avocado, halved, stoned
and sliced

35 g/1¼ oz rocket

salt and pepper

dressing
6 tbsp olive oil

3 tbsp lemon juice

1 tsp Dijon mustard

1–2 garlic cloves, crushed

salt and pepper

1. Bring a large saucepan of lightly salted water to the boil. Add the pasta, bring back to the boil and cook for 8–10 minutes, until tender but still firm to the bite. Meanwhile place all the ingredients for the dressing in a screw-top jar, and season to taste with salt and pepper. Place the lid on tightly and shake well to combine.

2. Drain the pasta and transfer to a large bowl. Add half the dressing, then toss together and leave to cool. Preheat the grill to high.

3. Grill the bacon for 2–3 minutes, turning until crispy. Transfer the bacon to a chopping board and slice into chunky pieces. Add the pieces to the bowl of pasta with the chicken, tomatoes, avocado and rocket. Pour the remaining dressing over the top and toss well. Serve immediately.

GOES WELL WITH

For an extra treat, serve with a side salad of spinach and baby sweetcorn dressed with a vinaigrette mixed with a little added diced avocado.

Honey & Chicken Pasta Salad

 SERVES 4    PREP TIME: 15 minutes   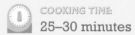 COOKING TIME: 25–30 minutes

nutritional information per serving	430 kcals, 9g fat, 1.5g saturated fat, 12g sugar, 0.5g salt

This delectable salad with its lovely combination of flavours is the perfect choice for an al fresco dinner on a warm summer's evening.

INGREDIENTS

250 g/9 oz dried fusilli
2 tbsp olive oil
1 onion, thinly sliced
1 garlic clove, crushed
400 g/14 oz skinless, boneless chicken breasts, thinly sliced
2 tbsp wholegrain mustard
2 tbsp clear honey
175 g/6 oz cherry tomatoes, halved
handful of rocket or mizuna leaves
fresh thyme leaves, to garnish
salt

dressing
3 tbsp olive oil
1 tbsp sherry vinegar
2 tsp clear honey
1 tbsp fresh thyme leaves
salt and pepper

1. To make the dressing, place all the ingredients in a small bowl and whisk together.

2. Bring a large saucepan of lightly salted water to the boil. Add the pasta, bring back to the boil and cook for 8–10 minutes, until tender but still firm to the bite.

3. Meanwhile, heat the oil in a large frying pan. Add the onion and garlic and fry for 5 minutes.

4. Add the chicken and cook, stirring frequently, for 3–4 minutes until cooked through. Stir the mustard and honey into the pan and cook for a further 2–3 minutes until the chicken and onion are golden brown and sticky.

5. Drain the pasta and transfer to a serving bowl. Pour over the dressing and toss. Stir in the chicken and onion and leave to cool.

6. Gently stir the tomatoes and rocket into the pasta. Serve immediately garnished with the thyme leaves.

1

3

4

Pasta & Chicken Medley

 SERVES 2    PREP TIME: 15 minutes    COOKING TIME: 10–15 minutes

nutritional information per serving   707 kcals, 36g fat, 6g saturated fat, 16g sugar, 0.4g salt

This is a delightfully elegant and truly delicious way to use up leftover cooked chicken.

INGREDIENTS

125–150 g/4½–5½ oz dried fusilli

2 tbsp mayonnaise

2 tsp pesto

1 tbsp soured cream or natural fromage frais

175 g/6 oz cooked skinless, boneless chicken, cut into strips

1–2 celery sticks, sliced diagonally

125 g/4½ oz black grapes, halved and deseeded

1 large carrot, cut into strips

salt and pepper

celery leaves, to garnish

dressing

1 tbsp white wine vinegar

3 tbsp extra virgin olive oil

salt and pepper

1. To make the dressing, whisk the vinegar and oil together, then season to taste with salt and pepper.

2. Bring a large saucepan of lightly salted water to the boil. Add the pasta, bring back to the boil and cook for 8–10 minutes, until tender but still firm to the bite. Drain thoroughly. Transfer to a bowl and mix in 1 tablespoon of the dressing while hot, then set aside until cold.

3. Combine the mayonnaise, pesto and soured cream in a bowl, and season to taste with salt and pepper.

4. Add the chicken, celery, grapes, carrot and the mayonnaise mixture to the pasta, and toss thoroughly. Check the seasoning, adding more salt and pepper if necessary.

5. Arrange the pasta mixture in a large serving bowl, garnish with the celery leaves and serve immediately with the reserved dressing.

1

3

4

Pappardelle with Chicken & Porcini Mushrooms

 SERVES 4

 PREP TIME: 40 minutes

 COOKING TIME: 1¼ hours

nutritional information per serving	519 kcals, 12g fat, 2g sat fat, 7.5g total sugars, 0.3g salt

Wild mushrooms are used extensively in Italian dishes and porcini mushrooms are the most popular. When using porcini, always soak them first in hot water for 30 minutes, then drain well before cooking.

INGREDIENTS

40 g/1½ oz dried porcini mushrooms

175 ml/6 fl oz hot water

800 g/1 lb 12 oz canned chopped tomatoes

1 fresh red chilli, deseeded and finely chopped

3 tbsp olive oil

350 g/12 oz skinless, boneless chicken, cut into thin strips

2 garlic cloves, finely chopped

350 g/12 oz dried pappardelle

salt and pepper

2 tbsp chopped fresh flat-leaf parsley, to garnish

1. Place the porcini in a small bowl, add the hot water and soak for 30 minutes. Meanwhile, place the tomatoes and their can juices in a heavy-based saucepan and break them up with a wooden spoon, then stir in the chilli. Bring to the boil, then reduce the heat and simmer, stirring occasionally, for 30 minutes, or until reduced.

2. Remove the mushrooms from their soaking liquid with a slotted spoon, reserving the liquid. Strain the liquid into the tomatoes through a sieve lined with muslin and simmer for a further 15 minutes.

3. Meanwhile, heat 2 tablespoons of the olive oil in a heavy-based frying pan. Add the chicken and cook, stirring frequently, for 3–4 minutes until cooked through. Stir in the mushrooms and garlic and cook for a further 5 minutes.

4. Bring a large saucepan of lightly salted water to the boil. Add the pasta, bring back to the boil and cook for 8–10 minutes, until tender but still firm to the bite. Drain well, then transfer to a warmed serving dish. Drizzle with the remaining olive oil and toss lightly. Stir the chicken mixture into the tomato sauce, season to taste with salt and pepper and spoon onto the pasta. Garnish with parsley and serve immediately.

Chicken Meatball Pasta

 SERVES 4    PREP TIME: 15 minutes    COOKING TIME: 35 minutes

nutritional information per serving	449 kcals, 11g fat, 2g saturated fat, 7g sugar, 0.6g salt

This lighter, more delicately flavoured twist on a familiar favourite is just as delicious and filling.

INGREDIENTS

3 tbsp olive oil

1 red onion, chopped

400 g/14 oz skinless, boneless chicken breasts, chopped

55 g/2 oz fresh white breadcrumbs

2 tsp dried oregano

1 garlic clove, crushed

400 g/14 oz canned chopped tomatoes

1 tbsp sun-dried tomato paste

300 ml/10 fl oz water

225 g/8 oz dried spaghetti or linguine

salt and pepper

Parmesan cheese shavings, to serve

1. Heat 1 tablespoon of the oil in a large frying pan and fry half the chopped onion for 5 minutes, until just softened. Leave to cool.

2. Place the chicken, breadcrumbs, oregano and the fried onion in a food processor or blender. Season to taste well with salt and pepper, and process for 2–3 minutes, until thoroughly combined. Shape into 24 meatballs.

3. Heat the remaining oil in the frying pan and fry the meatballs over a medium–high heat for 3–4 minutes, until golden brown. Remove and set aside.

4. Add the remaining onion and the garlic to the pan and fry for 5 minutes. Stir in the tomatoes, sun-dried tomato paste and water, and bring to the boil. Add the meatballs and simmer for 20 minutes. Season to taste with salt and pepper.

5. Meanwhile, bring a large saucepan of lightly salted water to the boil. Add the pasta, bring back to the boil and cook for 8–10 minutes, until tender but still firm to the bite. Drain thoroughly and toss with the meatballs and sauce. Serve immediately with Parmesan cheese shavings.

Chicken with Creamy Penne

 SERVES 2

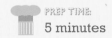 PREP TIME:
5 minutes

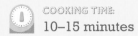 COOKING TIME:
10–15 minutes

nutritional information per serving	810 kcals, 30g fat, 15g sat fat, 4g total sugars, 0.3g salt

It is the pure simplicity of this delicately flavoured dish that makes it absolutely perfect.

INGREDIENTS

200 g/7 oz dried penne

1 tbsp olive oil

2 skinless, boneless chicken breasts

4 tbsp dry white wine

115 g/4 oz frozen peas

5 tbsp double cream

salt

4–5 tbsp chopped fresh parsley, to garnish

1. Bring a large saucepan of lightly salted water to the boil. Add the pasta, bring back to the boil and cook for 8–10 minutes, until tender but still firm to the bite.

2. Meanwhile, heat the oil in a frying pan, add the chicken and cook over a medium heat for about 4 minutes on each side, until cooked through and the juices run clear.

3. Pour in the wine and cook over a high heat until it has almost evaporated.

4. Drain the pasta. Add the peas, cream and pasta to the frying pan and stir well. Cover and simmer for 2 minutes. Garnish with chopped parsley and serve immediately.

1

2

4

GOES WELL WITH
A colourful chicory, orange and beetroot salad with a yogurt dressing would be the perfect partner for this creamy dish.

Spaghetti with Parsley Chicken

 SERVES 4    PREP TIME: 10 minutes    COOKING TIME: 35–40 minutes

nutritional information per serving	426 kcals, 16g fat, 8g saturated fat, 4g sugar, 0.5g salt

Subtly spiced with a hint of citrus, this zingy dish is a good choice for easy informal entertaining.

INGREDIENTS

1 tbsp olive oil

thinly pared rind of 1 lemon, cut into julienne strips

1 tsp finely chopped fresh ginger

1 tsp sugar

225 ml/8 fl oz chicken stock

250 g/9 oz dried spaghetti

55 g/2 oz butter

225 g/8 oz skinless, boneless chicken breasts, diced

1 red onion, finely chopped

leaves from 2 bunches of flat-leaf parsley

salt

1. Heat the oil in a heavy-based saucepan. Add the lemon rind and cook over a low heat, stirring frequently, for 5 minutes. Stir in the ginger and sugar, season to taste with salt and cook, stirring constantly, for a further 2 minutes. Pour in the stock, bring to the boil, then cook for 5 minutes, or until the liquid has reduced by half.

2. Meanwhile, bring a large saucepan of lightly salted water to the boil. Add the pasta, bring back to the boil and cook for 8–10 minutes, until tender but still firm to the bite.

3. Melt half the butter in a frying pan. Add the chicken and onion and cook, stirring frequently, for 5 minutes, or until cooked through and the juices run clear. Stir in the lemon and ginger mixture and cook for 1 minute. Stir in the parsley leaves and cook, stirring constantly, for a further 3 minutes.

4. Drain the pasta and transfer to a warmed serving dish, then add the remaining butter and toss well. Add the chicken sauce, toss again and serve immediately.

1

3

3

Cajun Chicken Pasta

 SERVES 6

 PREP TIME:
25 minutes

 COOKING TIME:
30 minutes

nutritional information per serving	793 kcals, 36g fat, 21g saturated fat, 7.5g sugar, 2.1g salt

Enjoy the spicy taste of New Orleans with this creamy mix of blackened chicken, pasta and fresh-tasting vegetables.

INGREDIENTS

150 g/5½ oz butter

6 skinless boneless chicken breasts

3 tbsp plain flour

450 ml/16 fl oz milk

225 ml/8 fl oz single cream

6 spring onions, chopped

450 g/1 lb dried pasta shapes, such as fusilli or farfalle

40 g/1½ oz Parmesan cheese, grated

diced tomatoes and stoned black olives, to garnish

spice mix

1 tbsp sweet paprika

1½ tsp salt

1 tsp onion powder

1 tsp garlic powder

1 tsp dried thyme

1 tsp cayenne pepper

½ tsp black pepper

½ tsp dried oregano

1. Heat a cast-iron frying pan over a high heat until very hot. Add 85 g/3 oz of the butter and melt over a low heat. Mix all the spice mix ingredients together in a shallow dish. Brush the chicken with the melted butter, dip into the spice mix to coat, shaking off the excess, and add to the pan. Cook for 5–8 minutes on each side until speckled with black, then remove the pan from the heat.

2. Meanwhile, melt 40 g/1½ oz of the remaining butter in a saucepan. Stir in the flour and cook, stirring constantly, for 1 minute. Remove the pan from the heat and whisk in the milk and cream, then return to the heat and bring to the boil, whisking constantly. Remove the pan from the heat.

3. Cut the chicken into thin strips and stir into the cream sauce with the spring onions. Return the pan to a medium–low heat and simmer, stirring frequently, for 20 minutes until the chicken is cooked through.

4. Meanwhile, bring a large saucepan of lightly salted water to the boil. Add the pasta, bring back to the boil and cook for 8–10 minutes, until tender but still firm to the bite. Drain, return to the pan, add the remaining butter and the cheese and toss well, then tip into a warmed serving dish. Spoon the Cajun chicken on top, garnish with diced tomatoes and olives and serve immediately.

1

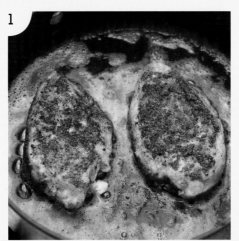

1

3

Penne with Chicken & Feta Cheese

 SERVES 4

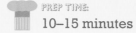 PREP TIME:
10–15 minutes

 COOKING TIME:
25–30 minutes

nutritional information per serving	700 kcals, 20g fat, 9g saturated fat, 4g sugar, 2.2g salt

The sharpness of the cheese gives a delicious piquancy to a dish that family and friends are sure to relish.

INGREDIENTS

2 tbsp olive oil

450 g/1 lb skinless, boneless chicken breasts, cut into thin strips

6 spring onions, chopped

225 g/8 oz feta cheese, diced

4 tbsp snipped fresh chives

450 g/1 lb dried penne

salt and pepper

1. Heat the oil in a heavy-based frying pan. Add the chicken and cook over a medium heat, stirring frequently, for 5–8 minutes, or until cooked through. Add the spring onions and cook for 2 minutes. Stir the feta cheese into the frying pan with half the chives and season to taste with salt and pepper.

2. Meanwhile, bring a large saucepan of lightly salted water to the boil. Add the pasta, bring back to the boil and cook for 8–10 minutes, until tender but still firm to the bite. Drain thoroughly, then transfer to a warmed serving dish.

3. Spoon the chicken mixture onto the pasta, toss lightly and serve immediately, garnished with the remaining chives.

GOES WELL WITH
Why not keep the Greek theme and serve this dish with a fresh-tasting Greek salad of olives, tomatoes and cucumber?

Spicy Chicken Pasta

 SERVES 4–6  PREP TIME:
25 minutes
plus marinating  COOKING TIME:
40 minutes

nutritional information per serving	500 kcals, 11g fat, 2g sat fat, 8g total sugars, 0.4g salt

You have to allow time for the chicken to marinate but this mouthwatering spicy dish is worth the wait.

INGREDIENTS

12 skinless boneless chicken thighs, cubed

1 tbsp groundnut oil

1 red pepper, deseeded and chopped

1 green pepper, deseeded and chopped

200 g/7 oz canned chopped tomatoes

450 g/1 lb dried spaghetti

salt

marinade

2 tbsp finely chopped spring onions, plus extra to garnish

1–2 chillies, deseeded (optional) and chopped

2 garlic cloves, finely chopped

1 tsp ground cinnamon

1 tsp ground allspice

pinch of grated nutmeg

2 tsp soft light brown sugar

2 tbsp groundnut oil

1 tbsp lime juice

1 tbsp white wine vinegar

salt and pepper

1. Put the chicken into a large, non-metallic dish. Mix all the marinade ingredients in a bowl, mashing everything together. Spoon the mixture over the chicken and rub it in with your hands. Cover the dish with clingfilm and leave to marinate in the refrigerator for at least 2 hours, preferably overnight.

2. Heat the oil in a saucepan, add the red pepper and green pepper and cook over a medium–low heat, stirring occasionally, for 5 minutes. Add the chicken and any remaining marinade and cook, stirring frequently, for 5 minutes until cooked through. Add the tomatoes, reduce the heat, cover and simmer, stirring occasionally, for 30 minutes. Check occasionally that the mixture is not drying out – if it is, add a little water.

3. Halfway through the chicken cooking time, bring a large saucepan of lightly salted water to the boil. Add the pasta, bring back to the boil and cook for 8–10 minutes, until tender but still firm to the bite.

4. Drain the pasta, tip it into the pan with the chicken and toss lightly. Transfer to warmed plates, garnish with the spring onion and serve immediately.

1

1

2

Pasta with Two Sauces

 SERVES 4    PREP TIME: 15 minutes   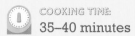 COOKING TIME: 35–40 minutes

nutritional information per serving	1099 kcals, 72g fat, 35g saturated fat, 10g sugar, 0.4g salt

This is a truly sophisticated dish that would be perfect to serve on a special occasion.

INGREDIENTS

2 tbsp olive oil

1 small onion, chopped

1 garlic clove, chopped

400 g/14 oz canned chopped tomatoes

2 tbsp chopped fresh parsley

1 tsp dried oregano

2 bay leaves

2 tbsp tomato purée

1 tsp sugar

55 g/2 oz unsalted butter

400 g/14 oz skinless, boneless chicken breasts, cut into thin slices

85 g/3 oz blanched almonds

300 ml/10 fl oz double cream

350 g/12 oz dried green tagliatelle

salt and pepper

fresh basil leaves, to garnish

1. To make the tomato sauce, heat the oil in a pan over a medium heat. Add the onion and cook until translucent. Add the garlic and cook for 1 minute. Stir in the tomatoes, parsley, oregano, bay leaves, tomato purée and sugar. Season to taste with salt and pepper, bring to the boil and simmer, uncovered, for 15–20 minutes, until reduced by half. Remove the pan from the heat and discard the bay leaves.

2. To make the chicken sauce, melt the butter in a frying pan over a medium heat. Add the chicken and almonds and cook for 5–6 minutes, or until the chicken is cooked through.

3. Meanwhile, bring the cream to the boil in a small pan over a low heat and boil for about 10 minutes, until reduced by almost half. Pour the cream over the chicken and almonds, stir and season to taste with salt and pepper. Reserve and keep warm.

4. Bring a large pan of lightly salted water to the boil over a medium heat. Add the pasta and cook for about 8–10 minutes, until tender but still firm to the bite. Drain and transfer to a warmed serving dish. Spoon over the tomato sauce and arrange the chicken sauce on top. Garnish with fresh basil leaves and serve immediately.

Turkey & Pasta Soup

 SERVES 4–6   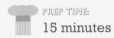 PREP TIME: 15 minutes    COOKING TIME: 30–35 minutes

nutritional information per serving	273 kcals, 3g fat, 0.5g saturated fat, 4.5g sugar, 1g salt

This quick and easy, colourful bowlful of pure comfort food is a great way to use up leftover turkey.

INGREDIENTS

1 tbsp olive oil

1 large onion, chopped

2 carrots, chopped

2 celery sticks, chopped

2 litres/3½ pints chicken stock or turkey stock

250–300 g/9–10½ oz cooked turkey, shredded

175 g/6 oz dried spaghetti, cooked

salt and pepper

1. Heat the oil in a large saucepan, add the onion, carrots and celery and cook over a low heat, stirring occasionally, for 8–10 minutes until the onion is just starting to colour.

2. Pour in the stock, increase the heat to medium and bring to the boil. Reduce the heat, season to taste with salt and pepper and simmer for 15 minutes.

3. Add the turkey and cooked spaghetti, stir well and simmer for a further 5 minutes. Taste and adjust the seasoning, if necessary, then ladle into warmed bowls and serve immediately.

FREEZING TIP
If you have more turkey, double the quantity and freeze half before adding the pasta. Store for up to 1 month and thaw at room temperature.

Mexican Spaghetti & Meatballs

 SERVES 4　　 PREP TIME: 20 minutes　　 COOKING TIME: 45 minutes

nutritional information per serving	715 kcals, 13g fat, 3g saturated fat, 9g sugar, 1g salt

This variation adds a touch of Latin vitality to what must be one of the most popular of all pasta recipes.

INGREDIENTS

1 tbsp olive oil, plus extra for greasing
450 g/1 lb fresh turkey mince
½–1 tsp dried crushed chillies
1 tbsp freshly grated Parmesan cheese
1 egg, lightly beaten
1 small onion, finely chopped
1–2 red chillies, deseeded (optional) and finely chopped
2 tostadas, crumbled
4 tbsp fresh breadcrumbs
350 g/12 oz dried spaghetti
salt

sauce
1 tbsp olive oil
1 small onion, chopped
1 garlic clove, finely chopped
1 chipotle chilli, finely chopped
1 tbsp tequila (optional)
400 g/14 oz canned chopped tomatoes
1 tbsp taco spice seasoning
1 tbsp chopped fresh coriander

1. Preheat the oven to 180°C/350°F/Gas Mark 4 and brush a baking sheet with oil. Mix together the turkey, dried chillies, cheese, egg, onion, fresh chillies, crumbled tostadas and breadcrumbs in a bowl and season to taste with salt. When the mixture is thoroughly combined, shape small pieces into balls, rolling them between the palms of your hands.

2. Put the balls on the prepared baking sheet and bake in the preheated oven for 20 minutes, then turn over and bake for a further 20 minutes.

3. Meanwhile, make the sauce. Heat the oil in a saucepan, add the onion, garlic and chilli and cook over a low heat, stirring occasionally, for 5 minutes. Add the tequila, if using, and cook for a further few minutes until the alcohol has evaporated, then add the tomatoes and stir in the spice seasoning. Simmer for 15 minutes.

4. Meanwhile, bring a large saucepan of lightly salted water to the boil. Add the pasta, bring back to the boil and cook for 8–10 minutes, until tender but still firm to the bite.

5. When the meatballs are cooked, remove from the oven, add to the sauce and stir in the coriander. Simmer for 5 minutes. Drain the pasta and tip it into a warmed serving dish. Add the meatballs and sauce and serve immediately.

Turkey Tetrazzini

 SERVES 4–6    PREP TIME: 15 minutes   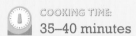 COOKING TIME: 35–40 minutes

nutritional information per serving	600 kcals, 31g fat, 16g sat fat, 2g total sugars, 1g salt

Named after a famous opera singer, this fabulous dish would certainly have a starring role when you're entertaining guests.

INGREDIENTS

3 tbsp olive oil

650 g/1 lb 7 oz turkey breast fillets, diced

115 g/4 oz butter, plus extra for greasing

2 tbsp plain flour

450 ml/16 fl oz chicken stock

dash of Tabasco sauce

1 egg yolk

2 tbsp medium sherry

125 ml/4 fl oz single cream

225 g/8 oz dried tagliatelle

225 g/8 oz mushrooms, sliced

55 g/2 oz freshly grated Parmesan cheese

55 g/2 oz fresh breadcrumbs

salt

1. Heat the oil in a frying pan, add the turkey and cook over a medium heat, stirring frequently, for 8–10 minutes until cooked through. Remove from the heat.

2. Melt half the butter in a saucepan, stir in the flour and cook, stirring constantly, for 1 minute. Remove from the heat and gradually stir in the stock. Return to the heat and bring to the boil, stirring constantly. Boil for 1 minute until thickened and smooth, then stir in the Tabasco sauce, season to taste with salt and remove from the heat.

3. Beat the egg yolk with a fork in a bowl, then beat in 2 tablespoons of the hot sauce. Stir the mixture into the sauce in the pan, then stir in the sherry, cream and turkey. Return the pan to a low heat and heat through, stirring constantly, but do not boil. Remove the pan from the heat.

4. Bring a large saucepan of lightly salted water to the boil. Add the pasta, bring back to the boil and cook for 8–10 minutes, until tender but still firm to the bite. Meanwhile, melt half the remaining butter in a small saucepan, add the mushrooms and cook, stirring occasionally, for 4–5 minutes. Add the mushrooms to the turkey mixture.

5. Preheat the grill. Grease a flameproof dish with butter. Drain the pasta. Make alternating layers of the turkey mixture and pasta in the dish. Sprinkle with the grated cheese and breadcrumbs, dot with the remaining butter and cook under the preheated grill until the top is golden and bubbling. Serve immediately.

Giant Pasta Shells with Turkey

 SERVES 4

 PREP TIME:
15 minutes

 COOKING TIME:
50 minutes

nutritional information per serving	724 kcals, 24g fat, 10g sat fat, 5g total sugars, 0.9g salt

This is a delicious way to serve stuffed pasta without having to spend time making fresh pasta dough.

INGREDIENTS

450 ml/16 fl oz passata

16 giant dried pasta shells

3 tbsp olive oil

1 onion, finely chopped

2 garlic cloves, finely chopped

450 g/1 lb fresh turkey mince

1 tbsp sun-dried tomato purée

1 tbsp finely chopped fresh flat-leaf parsley

225 g/8 oz mozzarella cheese, shredded

1–2 tsp black olive paste

salt and pepper

1. Pour the passata into a nylon strainer set over a bowl and set aside. Bring a large saucepan of lightly salted water to the boil. Add the pasta, bring back to the boil and cook for 8–10 minutes, until tender but still firm to the bite. Drain and set aside. Preheat the oven to 180°C/350°F/Gas Mark 4.

2. Meanwhile, heat 2 tablespoons of the oil in a frying pan, add the onion and half the garlic and cook over a low heat, stirring occasionally, for 5 minutes until soft. Add the turkey, increase the heat to medium and cook, stirring occasionally, for 8–10 minutes until cooked through. Stir in the tomato purée, parsley and half the cheese, season to taste with salt and pepper and remove the pan from the heat.

3. Tip the passata from the strainer into a bowl and stir in the olive paste and the remaining oil and garlic. Spread half this mixture over the base of an ovenproof dish. Divide the turkey mixture between the pasta shells and put them in the dish, meat-side up, then pour the remaining passata mixture over them. Cover the dish with foil and bake in the preheated oven for 25 minutes.

4. Remove the dish from the oven and discard the foil. Sprinkle the remaining cheese over the pasta, return the dish to the oven and bake for a further 5 minutes, until the cheese has melted. Serve immediately.

3

3

3

Turkey Pasta Primavera

 SERVES 4

 PREP TIME:
5 minutes

 COOKING TIME:
30–40 minutes

nutritional information
per serving   818 kcals, 41g fat, 22g saturated fat, 7g sugar, 0.6g salt

Primavera means spring and this is a fabulous way to make the most of the fresh-tasting young vegetables in season.

INGREDIENTS

25 g/1 oz butter
2 tbsp olive oil
2 shallots, finely chopped
1 garlic clove, finely chopped
500 g/1 lb 2 oz diced turkey
115 g/4 oz asparagus tips
2 carrots, thinly sliced diagonally
115 g/4 oz mushrooms, thinly sliced
1 tbsp chopped fresh sage
1 tbsp chopped fresh flat-leaf parsley
150 ml/5 fl oz dry white wine
175 ml/6 fl oz double cream
300 g/10½ oz dried pasta shapes, such as farfalle
55 g/2 oz freshly grated Parmesan cheese
salt and pepper

1. Melt the butter with the oil in a large frying pan, add the shallots and garlic and cook over a low heat, stirring occasionally, for 3–4 minutes until soft. Add the turkey, increase the heat to medium and cook, stirring frequently, for 6–8 minutes until cooked through.

2. Add the asparagus tips, carrots and mushrooms and cook, gently stirring occasionally, for 4–5 minutes until starting to soften, then add the herbs, wine and cream. Reduce the heat and simmer stirring occasionally, for 10–15 minutes until the vegetables are tender.

3. Meanwhile, bring a large saucepan of lightly salted water to the boil. Add the pasta, bring back to the boil and cook for 8–10 minutes, until tender but still firm to the bite. Drain the pasta, tip it into the pan of sauce, season to taste with salt and pepper and toss well. Transfer to a warmed serving dish, sprinkle with the cheese and serve immediately.

SOMETHING
DIFFERENT
This recipe is
almost infinitely
variable so you
can substitute your
favourite vegetables
and herbs.

Pasta with Chilli Barbecue Sauce

 SERVES 4

 PREP TIME:
20 minutes

 COOKING TIME:
30 minutes

nutritional information
per serving | 726 kcals, 21g fat, 6g saturated fat, 24g sugar, 1.2g salt

Even if it's pouring with rain outside, you can enjoy a touch of summer with this spicy barbecue-style pasta sauce.

INGREDIENTS

2 tbsp olive oil

2 garlic cloves, finely chopped

1 large onion, finely chopped

2 red peppers, deseeded and chopped

1–2 chillies, deseeded (optional) and finely chopped

450 g/1 lb fresh turkey mince

325 g/11½ oz canned sweetcorn kernels, drained

1 quantity Basic Tomato Sauce (see page 272)

2 tbsp Worcestershire sauce

1 tbsp red wine vinegar

1 tbsp soft light brown sugar

350 g/12 oz dried fusilli

2 tbsp chopped fresh parsley

salt and pepper

pickled chillies, drained and sliced, to garnish (optional)

1. Heat the oil in a frying pan, add the garlic, onion, red peppers and chillies and cook over a low heat, stirring occasionally, for 5 minutes. Increase the heat to medium, add the turkey and cook, stirring frequently, for 5–8 minutes until cooked through.

2. Stir in the sweetcorn, tomato sauce, Worcestershire sauce, vinegar and sugar. Season to taste with salt and pepper and simmer for 15 minutes.

3. Meanwhile, bring a large saucepan of lightly salted water to the boil. Add the pasta, bring back to the boil and cook for 8–10 minutes, until tender but still firm to the bite. Drain and tip into the pan of sauce. Add the parsley, taste and adjust the seasoning, if necessary, and remove from the heat. Transfer to a warmed serving dish and serve immediately, garnished with the pickled chillies, if using.

1

2

2

FREEZING TIP
You can freeze the sauce in an airtight container for up to 2 months, so why not make double the quantity?

Pasta with Harissa Turkey Meatballs

 SERVES 4  PREP TIME: 15 minutes 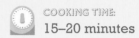 COOKING TIME: 15–20 minutes

nutritional information per serving	560 kcals, 10g fat, 3g sat fat, 7.5g total sugars, 0.7g salt

If you like spicy food, this North African-style dish is the perfect choice, and you can easily adjust the heat to suit you.

INGREDIENTS

350 g/12 oz fresh turkey mince

55 g/2 oz dry breadcrumbs

6 tbsp Greek-style yogurt

1 egg

½ tsp ground coriander

½ tsp ground cumin

½–1 tsp harissa

3 tbsp finely chopped parsley

350 g/12 oz dried spaghetti or tagliatelle

olive oil, for drizzling

salt and pepper

sauce

400 g/14 oz canned chopped tomatoes

1 small chilli, deseeded and finely chopped

¼ tsp ground cinnamon

½ tsp ground cumin

1. Preheat the oven to 200°C/400°F/Gas Mark 6. Line a baking sheet with baking paper.

2. Mix together the turkey, breadcrumbs, yogurt, egg, coriander, cumin, harissa and parsley in a bowl until thoroughly combined. Season to taste with salt and pepper. Shape the mixture into meatballs about the size of a golf ball and put them on the prepared baking sheet. Bake for 15 minutes until lightly browned.

3. Meanwhile, bring a large saucepan of lightly salted water to the boil. Add the pasta, bring back to the boil and cook for 8–10 minutes, until tender but still firm to the bite. Drain, transfer to a warmed dish, drizzle with oil and toss to coat.

4. Meanwhile, put all the sauce ingredients into a saucepan and simmer, stirring occasionally, for 5 minutes until thickened.

5. Remove the meatballs from the oven and add to the pasta. Pour the sauce over them and toss together. Serve immediately.

Fettuccine with Duck Sauce

 SERVES 4

 PREP TIME:
15 minutes

 COOKING TIME:
1¾ hours

nutritional information per serving	768 kcals, 27g fat, 6g saturated fat, 10g sugar, 1.3g salt

This unmistakably special occasion dish comes from northern Italy and would be a good choice for a celebration meal.

INGREDIENTS

4 tbsp olive oil

4 duck legs

1 shallot, finely chopped

1 leek, white part only, finely chopped

1 garlic clove, finely chopped

1 celery stick, finely chopped

1 carrot, finely chopped

4 pancetta or bacon slices, diced

1 tbsp finely chopped fresh flat-leaf parsley

1 bay leaf

5 tbsp dry white wine

400 g/14 oz canned chopped tomatoes

2 tbsp tomato purée

pinch of sugar

450 g/1 lb dried fettuccine

salt and pepper

freshly grated Parmesan cheese, to serve

1. Heat half the oil in a frying pan. Add the duck and cook over a medium heat, turning frequently, for 8–10 minutes, until golden brown. Using a slotted spoon, transfer to a large saucepan.

2. Wipe out the frying pan with kitchen paper, then add the remaining oil. Add the shallot, leek, garlic, celery, carrot and pancetta and cook over a low heat, stirring, for 10 minutes. Using a slotted spoon, transfer the mixture to the pan with the duck and stir in the parsley. Add the bay leaf and season to taste with salt and pepper. Pour in the wine and cook over a high heat, stirring occasionally, until reduced by half. Add the tomatoes, tomato purée and sugar and cook for a further 5 minutes. Pour in just enough water to cover and bring to the boil. Lower the heat, cover and simmer gently for 1 hour, until the duck is cooked through and tender.

3. Remove the pan from the heat and transfer the duck to a chopping board. Skim off the fat from the surface of the sauce and discard the bay leaf. Remove and discard the skin from the duck and cut the meat off the bones, then dice. Return the duck meat to the pan and keep warm.

4. Bring a large saucepan of lightly salted water to the boil. Add the pasta, bring back to the boil and cook for 8–10 minutes, until tender but still firm to the bite. Drain and place in a serving dish and spoon the duck sauce over. Sprinkle generously with Parmesan cheese and serve immediately.

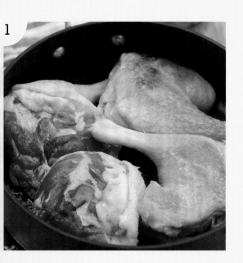

Venetian Duck with Spaghetti

 SERVES 4

 PREP TIME: 20 minutes

 COOKING TIME: 2 hours

nutritional information per serving	600 kcals, 16g fat, 5.5g saturated fat, 3.5g sugar, 0.4g salt

This is a simpler version of a traditional dish made with bigoli - thick spaghetti made with flour, butter and duck eggs - and preserved duck.

INGREDIENTS

4 duck legs
1 tbsp duck fat
1 tbsp butter
450 g/1 lb dried spaghetti
3 garlic cloves, peeled
juice and grated rind of ½ lemon
salt and pepper

1. Preheat the oven to 150°C/300°F/Gas Mark 2. Prick the skin on the duck legs all over with a skewer or needle and season well with salt. Put in a small roasting tin or ovenproof dish, fitting them snugly in a single layer. Roast in the preheated oven for 1½ hours, then increase the oven temperature to 200°C/400°F/Gas Mark 6 and roast for a further 15 minutes until the skin is light golden and crisp. Remove from the oven and leave to cool.

2. Remove the skin from the duck legs and roughly chop, then remove all the meat and roughly chop.

3. Heat a heavy-based saucepan over a medium heat, add the duck skin and meat with the duck fat and butter and cook over a medium–low heat for 10–12 minutes.

4. Meanwhile, bring a large saucepan of lightly salted water to the boil. Add the pasta, bring back to the boil and cook for 8–10 minutes, until tender but still firm to the bite.

5. Add the garlic to the pan with the duck and cook, stirring occasionally, for a few minutes, until the garlic starts to colour, then remove the pan from the heat. Remove and discard the garlic. Drain the pasta, add to the pan and return the pan to a medium heat. Toss together, then add the lemon juice, season to taste with pepper and toss again. Transfer to a warmed serving dish, sprinkle with the lemon rind and serve immediately.

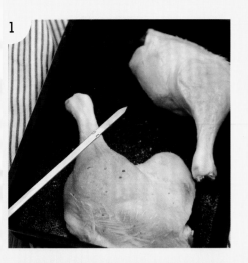

1

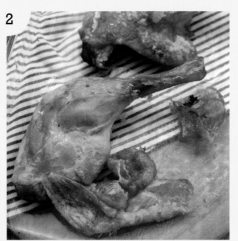

2

2

Salad Niçoise *118*

Spaghetti with Tuna & Parsley *120*

Spaghetti with Tuna Sauce *122*

Penne all'Arrabbiata with Smoked Cod *124*

Spaghetti & Cod *126*

Fettuccine with Sole & Monkfish *128*

Fusilli with Smoked Salmon & Dill *130*

Tagliatelle with Smoked Salmon & Rocket *132*

Sicilian Swordfish Pasta *134*

Linguine with Anchovies, Olives & Capers *136*

Linguine with Sardines *138*

Pasta Salad with Melon & Prawns *140*

Fettuccine & Prawn Parcels *142*

Springtime Pasta *144*

Garlic Prawns with Angel Hair Pasta *146*

Linguine with Prawns & Scallops *148*

Fusilli With Cajun Seafood Sauce *150*

Scallop Soup with Pasta *152*

Linguine with Clams in Tomato Sauce *154*

Penne with Squid & Tomatoes *156*

Mussel & Pasta Soup *158*

Conchiglie with Mussels *160*

Ravioli with Crabmeat & Ricotta *162*

Farfallini Buttered Lobster *164*

Fish & Seafood

Salad Niçoise

 SERVES 4–6    PREP TIME: 10 minutes    COOKING TIME: 20–25 minutes

nutritional information per serving	405 kcals, 14g fat, 3g sat fat, 4g total sugars, 1.2g salt

It is a matter of debate in culinary circles whether this Mediterranean salad should contain tomatoes, green beans, or hard-boiled eggs, but most renditions contain all these ingredients.

INGREDIENTS

350 g/12 oz dried conchiglie

2 tuna steaks, about 2 cm/¾ inch thick

olive oil, for brushing

250 g/9 oz French beans, topped and tailed

shop-bought garlic vinaigrette, to taste

2 hearts of lettuce, leaves separated

3 large hard-boiled eggs, halved

2 juicy tomatoes, cut into wedges

50 g/1¾ oz anchovy fillets in oil, drained

55 g/2 oz pitted black or Niçoise olives

salt and pepper

1. Bring a large saucepan of lightly salted water to the boil. Add the pasta, bring back to the boil and cook for 8–10 minutes, until tender but still firm to the bite. Drain and refresh in cold water.

2. Heat a ridged cast-iron griddle pan over a high heat. Brush the tuna steaks with oil on one side, place oiled-side down on the hot pan and chargrill for 2 minutes.

3. Lightly brush the top side of the tuna steaks with a little more oil. Turn the tuna steaks over, then season to taste with salt and pepper. Continue chargrilling for a further 2 minutes for rare or up to 4 minutes for well done. Leave to cool.

4. Meanwhile, bring a large saucepan of lightly salted water to the boil. Add the beans and return to the boil, then boil for 3 minutes. Drain and immediately transfer to a large bowl. Pour over the garlic vinaigrette and stir together.

5. To serve, line a serving dish with lettuce leaves. Lift the beans out of the bowl, leaving the excess dressing behind, and pile them in the centre of the platter. Break the tuna into large flakes and arrange it over the beans.

6. Arrange the hard-boiled eggs, tomatoes, anchovy fillets and olives on the platter. Drizzle over more vinaigrette, if required, and serve immediately.

Spaghetti with Tuna & Parsley

 SERVES 4

 PREP TIME: 10 minutes

 COOKING TIME: 15 minutes

nutritional information per serving	1109 kcals, 70g fat, 21g sat fat, 5g total sugars, 1.6g salt

This tasty dish is a great storecupboard stand-by that can be rustled up in no time at all.

INGREDIENTS

500 g/1 lb 2 oz dried spaghetti

25 g/1 oz butter

200 g/7 oz canned tuna in spring water, drained

55 g/2 oz canned anchovies, drained

250 ml/9 fl oz olive oil

1 large bunch of fresh flat-leaf parsley, roughly chopped

150 ml/5 fl oz crème fraîche

salt and pepper

1. Bring a large saucepan of lightly salted water to the boil. Add the pasta, bring back to the boil and cook for 8–10 minutes, until tender but still firm to the bite. Drain the spaghetti in a colander and return to the pan. Add the butter, toss thoroughly to coat and keep warm until required.

2. Flake the tuna into smaller pieces using two forks. Place the tuna in a food processor or blender with the anchovies, oil and parsley and process until the sauce is smooth. Pour in the crème fraîche and process for a few seconds to blend. Taste the sauce and season to taste with salt and pepper, if necessary.

3. Shake the pan of spaghetti over a medium heat for a few minutes, or until it is thoroughly warmed.

4. Pour the sauce over the spaghetti and toss. Serve immediately.

GOES WELL WITH
A mixed bean salad, perhaps including some fresh green beans, would be a perfect match for this dish.

Spaghetti with Tuna Sauce

 SERVES 4

 PREP TIME:
10 minutes

 COOKING TIME:
15 minutes

nutritional information
per serving

493 kcals, 8g fat, 1g saturated fat, 8g sugar, 0.8g salt

This is a terrific stand-by dish for those times when you have run out of ideas or are simply feeling tired.

INGREDIENTS

350 g/12 oz dried spaghetti

2 tbsp olive oil

1 garlic clove, peeled

1 onion, chopped

500 g/1 lb 2 oz tomatoes, chopped

400 g/14 oz canned tuna in spring water, drained and flaked

2 tbsp capers, rinsed (optional)

2 tbsp chopped fresh parsley, or 1 tbsp chopped fresh basil or pinch of dried oregano

salt and pepper

1. Bring a large saucepan of lightly salted water to the boil. Add the pasta, bring back to the boil and cook for 8–10 minutes, until tender but still firm to the bite.

2. Meanwhile, heat the oil in a separate saucepan and add the garlic. When it has begun to colour, remove and discard it. Add the onion and tomatoes to the pan and cook over a low heat, stirring occasionally, for 5 minutes.

3. Drain the pasta and tip it into the pan with the vegetables. Add the tuna and capers, if using, and toss over the heat for a few minutes until heated through. Remove from the heat, season to taste with salt and pepper, stir in the herbs and serve immediately.

SOMETHING DIFFERENT

You can add extra ingredients, such as a few chopped canned anchovies or sliced stoned olives, depending on what you have to hand.

Penne all'Arrabbiata
with Smoked Cod

SERVES 4–6

PREP TIME:
15 minutes

COOKING TIME:
25 minutes

nutritional information per serving	375 kcals, 13g fat, 2g saturated fat, 3.5g sugar, 2.1g salt

Arrabbiata means angry and describes the fierce heat from the local chillies in this dish from the Lazio region of Italy.

INGREDIENTS

6 tbsp olive oil

2 garlic cloves, finely chopped

2–3 dried chillies, finely chopped

500 g/1 lb 2 oz tomatoes, chopped

300 g/10½ oz dried penne

650 g/1 lb 7 oz smoked cod fillets, skinned and cut into large chunks

2 tbsp chopped fresh flat-leaf parsley

salt

1. Heat the oil in a large saucepan, add the garlic and chillies and cook over a low heat, stirring occasionally, for a few minutes, until the garlic is beginning to colour. Stir in the tomatoes, season to taste with salt and simmer for 15 minutes.

2. Bring a large saucepan of lightly salted water to the boil. Add the pasta, bring back to the boil and cook for 8–10 minutes, until tender but still firm to the bite.

3. Meanwhile, add the chunks of fish to the sauce, gently stir and simmer for a further 10 minutes.

4. Drain the pasta, tip it into the sauce and add the parsley. Toss together. Spoon into warmed bowls and serve immediately.

COOK'S NOTE

It's important that the tomatoes are sweet and ripe, so if they're not in season, substitute canned crushed tomatoes, also known as sugocasa.

Spaghetti & Cod

 SERVES 4

 PREP TIME:
10 minutes

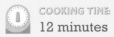 COOKING TIME:
12 minutes

nutritional information per serving	725 kcals, 39g fat, 6g saturated fat, 6g sugar, 0.3g salt

Although simplicity itself, this dish is surprisingly tasty and incredibly quick and easy to prepare and cook.

INGREDIENTS

300 g/10½ oz dried spaghetti

200 ml/7 fl oz extra virgin olive oil

1 garlic clove, peeled

450 g/1 lb cherry tomatoes, halved

pinch of crushed dried chillies (optional)

600 g/1 lb 5 oz cod fillets, skinned and cut into small chunks

salt and pepper

1. Bring a large saucepan of lightly salted water to the boil. Add the pasta, bring back to the boil and cook for 8–10 minutes, until tender but still firm to the bite. Reserve.

2. Meanwhile, put the oil into a large saucepan, add the garlic and cook over a low heat, stirring occasionally, for a few minutes until the garlic starts to brown, then remove and discard. Add the tomatoes to the pan and season with salt. Increase the heat to high and cook, tossing very occasionally, for 6–7 minutes until lightly browned and concentrated without disintegrating.

3. Add the chillies, if using, and the fish and cook, stirring gently, for 1–2 minutes. Add a ladleful of the cooking water from the pasta and taste and adjust the seasoning, if necessary. Drain the pasta, tip it into the sauce and toss together. Remove from the heat, spoon into warmed bowls and serve immediately.

2
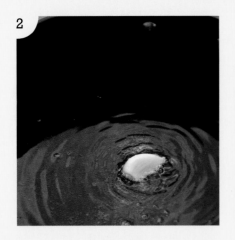

2

3

SOMETHING DIFFERENT
You could substitute another firm-fleshed white fish or large peeled prawns for the cod fillet.

Fettuccine with Sole & Monkfish

 SERVES 4  PREP TIME: 15 minutes  COOKING TIME: 50 minutes

nutritional information per serving	877 kcals, 23g fat, 12g saturated fat, 8.5g sugar, 1.3g salt

This is a wonderful dish not just for those who love fish but also for anyone who loves good food.

INGREDIENTS

450 g/1 lb lemon sole fillets
450 g/1 lb monkfish fillets
85 g/3 oz plain flour
85 g/3 oz unsalted butter
4 shallots, finely chopped
2 garlic cloves, crushed
1 carrot, diced
1 leek, finely chopped
300 ml/10 fl oz fish stock
300 ml/10 fl oz dry white wine
2 tsp anchovy extract
1 tbsp balsamic vinegar
450 g/1 lb dried fettuccine
salt and pepper
chopped fresh flat-leaf parsley, to garnish

1. Skin the lemon sole and monkfish fillets and cut into equal-size chunks.

2. Season the flour with salt and pepper and spread out 2 tablespoons of the mixture on a plate. Coat all the fish pieces with it, shaking off the excess. Melt the butter in a heavy-based saucepan or flameproof casserole dish. Add the fish, shallots, garlic, carrot and leek, and cook over a low heat, stirring frequently, for 10 minutes. Sprinkle in the remaining seasoned flour and cook, stirring constantly, for 1 minute.

3. Mix together the fish stock, wine, anchovy extract and balsamic vinegar in a jug and gradually stir into the fish mixture. Bring to the boil, stirring constantly, then reduce the heat and simmer gently for 35 minutes.

4. Meanwhile, bring a large saucepan of lightly salted water to the boil. Add the pasta, bring back to the boil and cook for 8–10 minutes, until tender but still firm to the bite. Drain and transfer to a warmed serving dish. Spoon the fish mixture onto the pasta, garnish with chopped parsley and serve immediately.

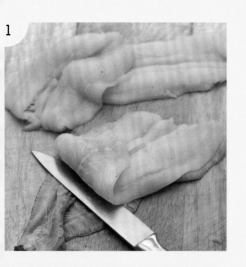

1

2

3

Fusilli with Smoked Salmon & Dill

 SERVES 4

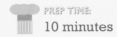 PREP TIME:
10 minutes

 COOKING TIME:
25–30 minutes

nutritional information
per serving | 1143 kcals, 76g fat, 44g sat fat, 5g total sugars, 2g salt

Not a traditional combination, but pasta and smoked salmon is now very much in fashion in Roman restaurants.

INGREDIENTS

450 g/1 lb dried fusilli

55 g/2 oz unsalted butter

1 small onion, finely chopped

6 tbsp dry white wine

450 ml/16 fl oz double cream

225 g/8 oz smoked salmon

2 tbsp snipped fresh dill, plus extra sprigs to garnish

1–2 tbsp lemon juice

salt and pepper

crusty bread, to serve

1. Bring a large saucepan of lightly salted water to the boil. Add the pasta, bring back to the boil and cook for 8–10 minutes, until tender but still firm to the bite.

2. Meanwhile, melt the butter in a heavy-based saucepan. Add the onion and cook over a low heat, stirring occasionally, for 5 minutes, or until softened. Add the wine, bring to the boil and continue boiling until reduced by two thirds. Pour in the cream and season to taste with salt and pepper. Bring to the boil, reduce the heat and simmer for 2 minutes, or until slightly thickened. Cut the smoked salmon into squares and stir into the pan with the snipped dill and lemon juice to taste.

3. Drain the pasta and transfer to a warmed serving dish. Add the smoked salmon mixture and toss well. Garnish with dill sprigs and serve immediately with the crusty bread.

GOES WELL WITH

For an extra special treat, serve this richly flavoured dish with a still or sparkling dry white wine, such as Frascati or Prosecco.

Tagliatelle with Smoked Salmon & Rocket

 SERVES 4

 PREP TIME:
5 minutes

 COOKING TIME:
15 minutes

nutritional information per serving	1141 kcals, 76g fat, 44g saturated fat, 5g sugar, 2g salt

This must be one of the easiest dishes to prepare while simultaneously being one of the most delicious to eat.

INGREDIENTS

350 g/12 oz dried tagliatelle

2 tbsp olive oil

1 garlic clove, finely chopped

115 g/4 oz smoked salmon, cut into thin strips

55 g/2 oz rocket

salt and pepper

1. Bring a large saucepan of lightly salted water to the boil. Add the pasta, bring back to the boil and cook for 8–10 minutes, until tender but still firm to the bite.

2. Just before the end of the cooking time, heat the olive oil in a heavy-based frying pan. Add the garlic and cook over a low heat, stirring constantly, for 1 minute. Do not allow the garlic to brown or it will taste bitter.

3. Add the salmon and rocket. Season to taste with pepper and cook, stirring constantly, for 1 minute. Remove the frying pan from the heat.

4. Drain the pasta and transfer to a warmed serving dish. Add the smoked salmon and rocket mixture, toss lightly and serve immediately.

GOES WELL WITH
Garlic bread would
complement this
delightfully without
detracting from the
delicate flavours
of the dish.

Sicilian Swordfish Pasta

 SERVES 4

 PREP TIME: 20 minutes

 COOKING TIME: 30 minutes

nutritional information per serving	441 kcals, 10g fat, 2g saturated fat, 6.5g sugar, 1.1g salt

Sicily is famous for its swordfish recipes which often also include other favourite ingredients, such as capers and olives.

INGREDIENTS

1 tbsp olive oil

4 garlic cloves, peeled

1 onion, chopped

8 black olives, stoned and chopped

4 cornichons (small gherkins), chopped

2 tbsp capers in salt, rinsed and chopped

300 g/10½ oz dried spaghetti or linguine

400g/14 oz canned chopped tomatoes

450 g/1 lb swordfish, cut into small chunks

basil leaves, to garnish

salt and pepper

1. Heat the oil in a deep frying pan and add the garlic. When the garlic begins to colour, remove and discard. Add the onion and cook over a low heat, stirring occasionally, for 8–10 minutes until light golden. Stir in the olives, cornichons and capers, season to taste with salt and pepper and cook, stirring occasionally, for 5 minutes.

2. Meanwhile, bring a large saucepan of lightly salted water to the boil. Add the pasta, bring back to the boil and cook for 8–10 minutes, until tender but still firm to the bite.

3. Add the tomatoes to the frying pan, increase the heat to medium and bring to the boil, stirring occasionally, then reduce the heat and simmer for 5 minutes. Add the swordfish chunks, cover and simmer gently for a further 5 minutes.

4. Drain the pasta and tip into a warmed serving dish. Top with the swordfish sauce and tear the basil leaves over it. Serve immediately.

COOK'S NOTE
Although it's an oily fish, swordfish dries out easily so simmer until it is just opaque to avoid overcooking.

Linguine with Anchovies, Olives & Capers

 SERVES 4    PREP TIME: 10 minutes    COOKING TIME: 30 minutes

nutritional information per serving	511 kcals, 17g fat, 2.5g saturated fat, 5g sugar, 1.6g salt

This quick and easy storecupboard supper has all the characteristics of a great Southern-Italian meal – piquant chillies, beautiful black olives and luscious tomatoes.

INGREDIENTS

3 tbsp olive oil

2 garlic cloves, finely chopped

10 anchovy fillets, drained and chopped

140 g/5 oz black olives, stoned and chopped

1 tbsp capers, rinsed

450 g/1 lb plum tomatoes, peeled, deseeded and chopped

400 g/14 oz dried linguine

salt and cayenne pepper

2 tbsp chopped fresh flat-leaf parsley, to garnish

1. Heat the oil in a heavy-based saucepan. Add the garlic and cook over a low heat, stirring frequently, for 2 minutes. Add the anchovies and mash them to a pulp with a fork.

2. Add the olives, capers and tomatoes and season to taste with cayenne pepper. Cover and simmer for 25 minutes.

3. Meanwhile, bring a saucepan of lightly salted water to the boil. Add the pasta, bring back to the boil and cook for 8–10 minutes, until tender but still firm to the bite.

4. Drain the pasta and transfer to a warmed serving dish. Spoon the anchovy sauce over the pasta and toss.

5. Garnish with chopped parsley and serve immediately.

COOK'S TIP:
Salted anchovies have a much better flavour than canned fillets, but are not so widely available. If you can find them, soak them in cold water for 30 minutes, then pat dry with paper towels before using.

Linguine with Sardines

 SERVES 4

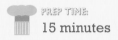 PREP TIME:
15 minutes

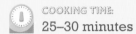 COOKING TIME:
25–30 minutes

nutritional information per serving	624 kcals, 27g fat, 5g saturated fat, 3g sugar, 0.3g salt

This classic Sicilian dish with its robust flavours is filling, delicious and a great addition to a healthy diet.

INGREDIENTS

8 sardines, filleted, washed and dried

4 tbsp olive oil

3 garlic cloves, sliced

1 tsp chilli flakes

1 fennel bulb, trimmed and thinly sliced

350 g/12 oz dried linguine

½ tsp finely grated lemon rind

1 tbsp lemon juice

2 tbsp toasted pine kernels

2 tbsp chopped fresh parsley

salt and pepper

1. Roughly chop the sardines into large pieces and reserve.

2. Heat 2 tablespoons of the oil in a large frying pan over a medium-high heat and add the garlic and chilli flakes. Cook for 1 minute, then add the fennel. Cook, stirring occasionally, for 4–5 minutes, or until soft. Reduce the heat, add the sardine pieces and cook for a further 3–4 minutes.

3. Meanwhile, bring a large saucepan of lightly salted water to the boil. Add the pasta, bring back to the boil and cook for 8–10 minutes, until tender but still firm to the bite. Drain thoroughly and return to the pan.

4. Add the lemon rind, lemon juice, pine kernels and parsley to the sardine mixture and toss. Season to taste with salt and pepper.

5. Add to the pasta with the remaining oil and toss. Transfer to a warmed serving dish and serve immediately.

Pasta Salad with Melon & Prawns

 SERVES 6

 PREP TIME:
25 minutes
plus chilling

 COOKING TIME:
15 minutes

nutritional information
per serving | 334 kcals, 11g fat, 1.5g sat fat, 15g total sugars, 1.2g salt

This lovely salad looks really spectacular and tastes fabulous so would be a great choice for a special occasion.

INGREDIENTS

225 g/8 oz dried green fusilli

5 tbsp extra virgin olive oil

450 g/1 lb cooked prawns

1 Charentais melon

1 Galia melon

1 tbsp red wine vinegar

1 tsp Dijon mustard

pinch of caster sugar

1 tbsp chopped fresh flat-leaf parsley

1 tbsp chopped fresh basil, plus extra sprigs to garnish

1 oakleaf or quattro stagioni lettuce, shredded

salt and pepper

1. Bring a large saucepan of lightly salted water to the boil. Add the pasta, bring back to the boil and cook for 8–10 minutes, until tender but still firm to the bite. Drain, toss with 1 tablespoon of the oil and leave to cool.

2. Meanwhile, peel and devein the prawns, then place them in a large bowl. Halve both the melons and scoop out the seeds with a spoon. Using a melon baller or teaspoon, scoop out balls of the flesh and add them to the prawns.

3. Whisk together the remaining oil, the vinegar, mustard, sugar, parsley and basil in a small bowl. Season to taste with salt and pepper. Add the cooled pasta to the prawn and melon mixture and toss lightly to mix, then pour in the dressing and toss again. Cover with clingfilm and chill in the refrigerator for 30 minutes.

4. Make a bed of shredded lettuce on a serving plate. Spoon the pasta salad on top, garnish with basil sprigs and serve immediately.

Fettuccine & Prawn Parcels

 SERVES 4    PREP TIME: 10 minutes    COOKING TIME: 20–25 minutes

nutritional information
per serving   769 kcals, 23g fat, 1g saturated fat, 2.5g sugar, 1.3g salt

Pasta al cartoccio - in a parcel - has become very fashionable in restaurants throughout Italy and abroad.

INGREDIENTS

450 g/1 lb dried fettuccine

150 ml/5 fl oz Pesto (see page 276)

4 tsp extra virgin olive oil

750 g/1 lb 10 oz large raw prawns, peeled and deveined

2 garlic cloves, crushed

125 ml/4 fl oz dry white wine

salt and pepper

1. Preheat the oven to 200°C/400°F/Gas Mark 6. Cut out four 30-cm/12-inch squares of greaseproof paper. Bring a large saucepan of lightly salted water to the boil. Add the pasta, bring back to the boil and cook for 2–3 minutes, or until just softened. Drain and reserve.

2. Mix the fettuccine and half of the pesto together in a bowl. Spread out the paper squares and place 1 teaspoon of oil in the centre of each. Divide the fettuccine between the squares, then divide the prawns and place on top of the fettuccine. Mix the remaining pesto and the garlic together and spoon it over the prawns. Season each parcel to taste with salt and pepper and sprinkle with the white wine. Dampen the edges of the greaseproof paper and wrap the parcels loosely, twisting the edges to seal.

3. Place the parcels on a baking sheet and bake in the preheated oven for 10–15 minutes. Transfer the parcels to warmed plates and serve immediately.

GOES WELL WITH

A salad of broad beans and crumbled feta dressed with a minty lemon vinaigrette has the perfect colour, texture and flavour to partner these parcels.

Springtime Pasta

 SERVES 4    PREP TIME: 15 minutes   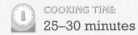 COOKING TIME: 25–30 minutes

nutritional information per serving	611 kcals, 27g fat, 7g saturated fat, 6g sugar, 0.4g salt

Globe artichokes grow wild in Sicily and are cultivated throughout Italy, but they are always considered a speciality of Roman cooking.

INGREDIENTS

2 tbsp lemon juice

4 baby globe artichokes

7 tbsp olive oil

2 shallots, finely chopped

2 garlic cloves, finely chopped

2 tbsp chopped fresh flat-leaf parsley

2 tbsp chopped fresh mint

350 g/12 oz dried rigatoni

25 g/1 oz unsalted butter

12 large raw prawns, peeled and deveined

salt and pepper

1. Fill a bowl with cold water and add the lemon juice. Prepare the artichokes one at a time. Cut off the stems and trim away any tough outer leaves. Cut across the tops of the leaves. Slice in half lengthways and remove the central fibrous chokes, then cut lengthways into 5-mm/¼-inch thick slices. Immediately place the slices in the bowl of acidulated water to prevent discoloration.

2. Heat 5 tablespoons of the oil in a heavy-based frying pan. Drain the artichoke slices and pat dry with kitchen paper. Add them to the frying pan with the shallots, garlic, parsley and mint and cook over a low heat, stirring frequently, for 10–12 minutes, until tender.

3. Meanwhile, bring a large saucepan of lightly salted water to the boil. Add the pasta, bring back to the boil and cook for 8–10 minutes, until tender but still firm to the bite.

4. Melt the butter in a small frying pan and add the prawns. Cook, stirring occasionally, for 2–3 minutes, until opaque and firm to the touch. Season to taste with salt and pepper.

5. Drain the pasta and tip it into a bowl. Add the remaining oil and toss. Add the artichoke mixture and the prawns and toss again. Spoon into warmed bowls and serve immediately.

Garlic Prawns with Angel Hair Pasta

 SERVES 4

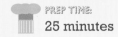 PREP TIME: 25 minutes

 COOKING TIME: 45 minutes

nutritional information per serving	593 kcals, 21g fat, 4g saturated fat, 4g sugar, 0.6g salt

Truly a dish made in heaven, this is a special treat for a celebration and is ideal for easy – and impressive – entertaining.

INGREDIENTS

500 g/1 lb 2 oz raw tiger prawns

1 avocado

2 tbsp lemon juice

4 tbsp olive oil

1 onion, finely chopped

350 ml/12 fl oz dry white wine

1 bouquet garni

300 g/10½ oz dried angel hair pasta

3 large garlic cloves, finely chopped

salt and pepper

1. Peel the prawns, reserving the heads and shells. Cut along the back of each prawn and remove the black vein. Peel, stone and slice the avocado, put into a bowl and toss with the lemon juice.

2. Heat half the oil in a saucepan, add the onion and cook over a low heat, stirring occasionally, for 5 minutes. Add the prawn heads and shells and cook, mashing with a wooden spoon, for 5 minutes, then add the wine and bouquet garni. Increase the heat to medium and bring to the boil. Reduce the heat and simmer for 20 minutes.

3. Meanwhile, bring a large saucepan of lightly salted water to the boil. Add the pasta, bring back to the boil and cook for 3 minutes. Remove from the heat, drain and set aside.

4. Remove and discard the bouquet garni. Transfer the prawn shell mixture to a food processor or blender and process until combined, then strain into a clean saucepan. Bring to the boil, then add the pasta and cook for a few more minutes, until the pasta is tender but still firm to the bite.

5. Meanwhile, heat the remaining oil in a frying pan over a medium heat. Add the prawns and cook, stirring frequently, for 2–3 minutes until opaque and firm to the touch. Add the garlic and cook, stirring frequently for a further minute. Season to taste with salt and pepper and remove from the heat.

6. Drain the pasta, toss with the avocado and transfer to a serving dish. Top with the prawns and serve immediately.

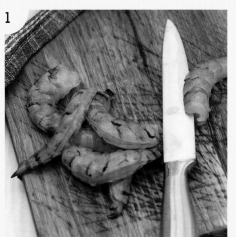

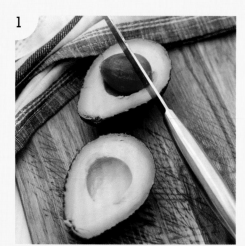

Linguine with Prawns & Scallops

 SERVES 6

 PREP TIME:
15 minutes

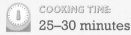 COOKING TIME:
25–30 minutes

nutritional information
per serving

514 kcals, 10g fat, 3g saturated fat, 3g sugar, 0.8g salt

This impressive dish from the coastal regions of northern Italy is a real treat for lovers of seafood.

INGREDIENTS

450 g/1 lb raw prawns

25 g/1 oz butter

2 shallots, finely chopped

225 ml/8 fl oz dry white vermouth

350 ml/12 fl oz water

450 g/1 lb dried linguine

2 tbsp olive oil

450 g/1 lb prepared scallops, thawed if frozen

2 tbsp snipped fresh chives

salt and pepper

1. Peel and devein the prawns, reserving the shells. Melt the butter in a heavy-based frying pan. Add the shallots and cook over a low heat, stirring occasionally, for 5 minutes, or until softened. Add the prawn shells and cook, stirring constantly, for 1 minute. Pour in the vermouth and cook, stirring, for 1 minute. Add the water, bring to the boil, then reduce the heat and simmer for 10 minutes, or until the liquid has reduced by half. Remove the pan from the heat.

2. Bring a large saucepan of lightly salted water to the boil. Add the pasta, bring back to the boil and cook for 8–10 minutes, until tender but still firm to the bite.

3. Meanwhile, heat the oil in a separate heavy-based frying pan. Add the scallops and prawns and cook, stirring frequently, for 2 minutes, or until the scallops are opaque and the prawns have changed colour. Strain the prawn-shell stock into the frying pan. Drain the pasta and add to the frying pan with the chives. Season to taste with salt and pepper. Toss well over a low heat for 1 minute, then serve.

1

1

3

GOES WELL WITH
Serve with
lightly steamed
samphire or
asparagus,
tossed with
a little melted
butter.

Fusilli with Cajun Seafood Sauce

 SERVES 4

 PREP TIME:
15 minutes

 COOKING TIME:
25 minutes

nutritional information per serving	1095 kcals, 64g fat, 36g saturated fat, 7g sugar, 2.1g salt

If you love hot spices and rich mixtures of cream and cheese, then this is the dish for you.

INGREDIENTS

500 ml/18 fl oz whipping cream

8 spring onions, thinly sliced

55 g/2 oz chopped fresh flat-leaf parsley

1 tbsp chopped fresh thyme

½ tbsp pepper

½–1 tsp dried chilli flakes

1 tsp salt

450 g/1 lb dried fusilli

40 g/1½ oz freshly grated Gruyère cheese

20 g/¾ oz freshly grated Parmesan cheese

2 tbsp olive oil

225 g/8 oz raw prawns, peeled and deveined

225 g/8 oz scallops, sliced

1 tbsp shredded fresh basil, to garnish

1. Heat the cream in a large saucepan over a medium heat, stirring constantly. When almost boiling, reduce the heat and add the spring onions, parsley, thyme, pepper, chilli flakes and salt. Simmer for 7–8 minutes, stirring, until thickened. Remove from the heat.

2. Bring a large saucepan of lightly salted water to the boil. Add the pasta, bring back to the boil and cook for 8–10 minutes, until tender but still firm to the bite. Drain and return to the pan. Add the cream mixture and the cheeses to the pasta. Toss over a low heat until the cheeses have melted. Transfer to a warmed serving dish.

3. Heat the oil in a large frying pan over a medium–high heat. Add the prawns and scallops. Cook for 2–3 minutes, until the prawns have turned opaque and are firm to the touch.

4. Pour the seafood over the pasta and toss to mix. Sprinkle with the basil and serve immediately.

Scallop Soup with Pasta

 SERVES 6

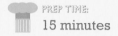 PREP TIME:
15 minutes

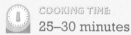 COOKING TIME:
25–30 minutes

nutritional information **per serving**	444 kcals, 15g fat, 8g sat fat, 5g total sugars, 1.6g salt

If you're planning a formal dinner party, this elegant soup would be the ideal first course.

INGREDIENTS

500 g/1 lb 2 oz shelled scallops

350 ml/12 fl oz milk

1.5 litres/2¾ pints vegetable stock

250 g/9 oz frozen petits pois

175 g/6 oz dried taglialini

70 g/2½ oz butter

2 spring onions, finely chopped

175 ml/6 fl oz dry white wine

3 slices of prosciutto, cut into thin strips

salt and pepper

chopped fresh flat-leaf parsley, to garnish

crusty baguette, to serve

1. Slice the scallops in half horizontally and season to taste with salt and pepper.

2. Pour the milk and stock into a saucepan, add a pinch of salt and bring to the boil. Add the petits pois and pasta, bring back to the boil and cook for 8–10 minutes, until the pasta is tender but still firm to the bite.

3. Meanwhile, melt the butter in a frying pan. Add the spring onions and cook over a low heat, stirring occasionally, for 3 minutes. Add the scallops and cook for 45 seconds on each side. Pour in the wine, add the prosciutto and cook for 2–3 minutes.

4. Stir the scallop mixture into the soup, taste and adjust the seasoning, if necessary, and garnish with the parsley. Serve immediately with the baguette.

1

2

3

GOES WELL WITH
Serve with bruschetta - thick slices of lightly toasted rustic bread or baguette, rubbed with garlic and drizzled with olive oil.

Linguine with Clams in Tomato Sauce

 SERVES 4

 PREP TIME: 20 minutes

 COOKING TIME: 35 minutes

nutritional information per serving	522 kcals, 11.5g fat, 2g saturated fat, 9g sugar, 0.7g salt

This Neapolitan speciality features three of the city's favourite ingredients - pasta, tomatoes and clams.

INGREDIENTS

1 kg/2 lb 4 oz live clams, scrubbed

225 ml/8 fl oz dry white wine

2 garlic cloves, roughly chopped

4 tbsp chopped fresh flat-leaf parsley

2 tbsp olive oil

1 onion, chopped

8 plum tomatoes, peeled, deseeded and chopped

1 fresh red chilli, deseeded and chopped

350 g/12 oz dried linguine

salt and pepper

1. Discard any clams with broken shells or any that refuse to close when tapped. Pour the wine into a large heavy-based saucepan and add the garlic, half the parsley and the clams. Cover and cook over a high heat, shaking the pan occasionally, for 5 minutes, or until the shells have opened. Remove the clams with a slotted spoon, reserving the cooking liquid. Discard any that remain closed and remove half of the remainder from their shells. Keep the shelled and unshelled clams in separate covered bowls. Strain the cooking liquid through a muslin-lined sieve and reserve.

2. Heat the oil in a heavy-based saucepan. Add the onion and cook over a low heat for 5 minutes, or until softened. Add the tomatoes, chilli and reserved cooking liquid and season to taste with salt and pepper. Bring to the boil, partially cover the pan and simmer for 20 minutes.

3. Meanwhile, bring a large saucepan of lightly salted water to the boil. Add the pasta, bring back to the boil and cook for 8–10 minutes, until tender but still firm to the bite. Drain and transfer to a warmed serving dish.

4. Stir the shelled clams into the tomato sauce and heat through gently for 2–3 minutes. Pour over the pasta and toss. Garnish with the clams in their shells and remaining parsley. Serve immediately.

Penne with Squid & Tomatoes

 SERVES 4 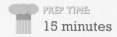 PREP TIME: 15 minutes   COOKING TIME: 30–35 minutes

nutritional information per serving	493 kcals, 19g fat, 3g saturated fat, 8g sugar, 0.6g salt

The availability of prepared squid makes this richly flavoured southern Italian dish quick and trouble-free.

INGREDIENTS

225 g/8 oz dried penne

350 g/12 oz prepared squid

6 tbsp olive oil

2 onions, sliced

225 ml/8 fl oz fish or chicken stock

150 ml/5 fl oz full-bodied red wine

400 g/14 oz canned chopped tomatoes

2 tbsp tomato purée

1 tbsp chopped fresh marjoram

1 bay leaf

salt and pepper

2 tbsp chopped fresh parsley, to garnish

1. Bring a large saucepan of lightly salted water to the boil. Add the pasta, bring back to the boil and cook for 3 minutes, then drain and reserve until required. With a sharp knife, cut the squid into strips.

2. Heat the oil in a large saucepan. Add the onions and cook over a low heat, stirring occasionally, for 5 minutes, or until softened. Add the squid and stock, bring to the boil and simmer for 3 minutes. Stir in the wine, tomatoes and their can juices, tomato purée, marjoram and bay leaf. Season to taste with salt and pepper. Bring to the boil and cook for 5 minutes, or until slightly reduced.

3. Add the pasta, return to the boil and simmer for 5–7 minutes, or until the pasta is tender but still firm to the bite. Remove and discard the bay leaf. Transfer to a warmed serving dish, garnish with the parsley and serve immediately.

1

2

2

GOES WELL WITH
A simple salad of mixed leaves and fresh herbs would be a refreshing accompaniment to this rich and substantial dish.

Mussel & Pasta Soup

 SERVES 4   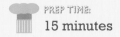 PREP TIME: 15 minutes    COOKING TIME: 35 minutes

nutritional information per serving	996 kcals, 75g fat, 41g saturated fat, 4g sugar, 1.3g salt

This rich and filling soup is full of flavour and would make a great weekend lunch with some crusty bread.

INGREDIENTS

750 g/1 lb 10 oz mussels, scrubbed and debearded

2 tbsp olive oil

100 g/3½ oz butter

55 g/2 oz rindless streaky bacon, chopped

1 onion, chopped

2 garlic cloves, finely chopped

55 g/2 oz plain flour

3 potatoes, thinly sliced

115 g/4 oz dried farfalle

300 ml/10 fl oz double cream

1 tbsp lemon juice

2 egg yolks

salt and pepper

2 tbsp finely chopped fresh parsley, to garnish

1. Discard any mussels with broken shells or any that refuse to close when tapped. Bring a large heavy-based saucepan of water to the boil. Add the mussels and oil and season to taste with pepper. Cover tightly and cook over a high heat for 5 minutes, or until the mussels have opened. Remove the mussels with a slotted spoon, discarding any that remain closed. Strain the cooking liquid through a muslin-lined sieve and reserve 1.2 litres/2 pints.

2. Melt the butter in a saucepan. Add the bacon, onion and garlic and cook over a low heat, stirring occasionally, for 5 minutes. Stir in the flour and cook, stirring, for 1 minute. Gradually stir in all but 2 tablespoons of the reserved cooking liquid and bring to the boil, stirring constantly. Add the potato slices and simmer for 5 minutes. Add the pasta and simmer for a further 10 minutes.

3. Stir in the cream and lemon juice and season to taste with salt and pepper. Add the mussels. Mix the egg yolks and the remaining mussel cooking liquid together, then stir the mixture into the soup and cook for 4 minutes, until thickened.

4. Ladle the soup into warmed bowls, garnish with chopped parsley and serve immediately.

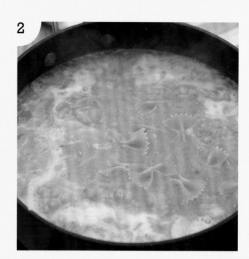

Conchiglie with Mussels

 SERVES 6

 PREP TIME:
15–20 minutes

 COOKING TIME:
25–30 minutes

nutritional information per serving	724 kcals, 45g fat, 27g saturated fat, 5g sugar, 0.9g salt

Mussels and pasta make a terrific combination and are popular in all coastal regions of Italy.

INGREDIENTS

1.25 kg/2 lb 12 oz live mussels, scrubbed and debearded

225 ml/8 fl oz dry white wine

2 large onions, chopped

115 g/4 oz unsalted butter

6 large garlic cloves, finely chopped

5 tbsp chopped fresh parsley

300 ml/10 fl oz double cream

400 g/14 oz dried conchiglie

salt and pepper

1. Discard any mussels with broken shells or any that refuse to close when tapped. Place the mussels in a large heavy-based saucepan, together with the wine and half of the onions. Cover and cook over a medium heat, shaking the saucepan frequently, for 2–3 minutes, or until the shells open. Remove the saucepan from the heat. Drain the mussels and reserve the cooking liquid. Discard any mussels that remain closed. Strain the cooking liquid through a muslin-lined sieve into a bowl and reserve.

2. Melt the butter in a saucepan. Add the remaining onions and cook until translucent. Stir in the garlic and cook for 1 minute. Gradually stir in the reserved cooking liquid. Stir in the parsley and cream and season to taste with salt and pepper. Bring to simmering point over a low heat.

3. Meanwhile, bring a large saucepan of lightly salted water to the boil. Add the pasta, bring back to the boil and cook for 8–10 minutes, until tender but still firm to the bite. Drain and keep warm.

4. Reserve a few mussels for the garnish and remove the remainder from their shells. Stir the shelled mussels into the cream sauce and warm briefly. Transfer the pasta to a warmed dish. Pour over the sauce and toss. Garnish with the reserved mussels and serve immediately.

Ravioli with Crabmeat & Ricotta

 SERVES 4

 PREP TIME:
25 minutes
plus resting

 COOKING TIME:
10 minutes

nutritional information per serving	570 kcals, 28g fat, 14g saturated fat, 2g sugar, 2.2g salt

Home-made ravioli are a special treat and these would make an impressive first course for a dinner party.

INGREDIENTS

300 g/10½ oz type 00 pasta flour or strong white flour

1 tsp salt

3 eggs, beaten

70 g/2½ oz butter, melted

filling

175 g/6 oz white crabmeat

175 g/6 oz ricotta cheese

finely grated rind of 1 lemon

pinch of dried chilli flakes

2 tbsp chopped fresh flat-leaf parsley

salt and pepper

1. Sift the flour and salt onto a board or work surface, make a well in the centre and add the eggs. Stir with a fork to gradually incorporate the flour into the liquid to form a dough. Knead for about 5 minutes, until the dough is smooth. Wrap in clingfilm and leave to rest for 20 minutes.

2. For the filling, stir together the crabmeat, ricotta, lemon rind, chilli flakes and parsley. Season to taste with salt and pepper.

3. Roll the dough with a pasta machine or by hand to a thickness of about 3 mm/⅛ inch and cut into 32 x 6-cm/2½-inch squares.

4. Place a spoonful of the filling in the centre of half the squares. Brush the edges with water and place the remaining squares on top, pressing to seal.

5. Bring a saucepan of lightly salted water to the boil. Add the ravioli, bring back to the boil and cook for about 3 minutes, until tender but still firm to the bite. Drain well. Drizzle the melted butter over the ravioli, sprinkle with pepper and serve immediately.

Farfallini Buttered Lobster

 SERVES 4  PREP TIME: 30–35 minutes  COOKING TIME: 30–35 minutes

nutritional information per serving	764 kcals, 34g fat, 20g saturated fat, 3g sugar, 1.6g salt

Wonderfully luxurious, this has to be the ultimate pasta dish for a very special occasion.

INGREDIENTS

2 lobsters (about 700 g/1 lb 9 oz each), split into halves

juice and grated rind of 1 lemon

115 g/4 oz butter

4 tbsp fresh white breadcrumbs

2 tbsp brandy

5 tbsp double cream or crème fraîche

450 g/1 lb dried farfallini

55 g/2 oz freshly grated Parmesan cheese

salt and pepper

lemon wedges and fresh dill sprigs, to garnish

1. Preheat the oven to 160°C/325°F/Gas Mark 3. Discard the stomach sac, vein and gills from each lobster. Remove the meat from the tail and chop. Crack the claws and legs, remove the meat and chop. Transfer the meat to a bowl and add the lemon juice and lemon rind. Clean the shells and place in the oven to dry out.

2. Melt 25 g/1 oz of the butter in a frying pan. Add the breadcrumbs and cook for 3 minutes, until crisp and golden brown. Melt the remaining butter in a separate saucepan. Add the lobster meat and heat through gently. Add the brandy and cook for a further 3 minutes, then add the cream and season to taste with salt and pepper.

3. Meanwhile, bring a large saucepan of lightly salted water to the boil. Add the pasta, bring back to the boil and cook for 8–10 minutes, until tender but still firm to the bite. Drain and spoon the pasta into the clean lobster shells.

4. Preheat the grill to medium. Spoon the buttered lobster on top of the pasta and sprinkle with a little Parmesan cheese and the breadcrumbs. Grill for 2–3 minutes, or until golden brown. Transfer the lobster shells to a warmed plate, garnish with the lemon wedges and dill sprigs and serve immediately.

Fresh Tomato Soup with Pasta *168*

Hearty Bean & Pasta Soup *170*

Potato & Pasta Soup with Pesto *172*

Tomato, Olive & Mozzarella Pasta Salad *174*

Chilli Broccoli Pasta *176*

Double Cheese Macaroni *178*

Penne with Asparagus & Blue Cheese *180*

Rigatoni with Peppers & Goat's Cheese *182*

Pasta with Camembert *184*

Creamy Asparagus & Brie Tagliatelle *186*

Linguine with Lemon, Chilli & Spinach *188*

Spaghetti Olio E Aglio *190*

Pasta with Leek & Butternut Squash *192*

Conchiglie with Marinated Artichoke *194*

Spicy Aubergine, Chickpea & Coriander Penne *196*

Ziti with Rocket *198*

Garlic Mushroom Pasta *200*

Linguine with Wild Mushrooms *202*

Macaroni with Chickpeas, Herbs & Garlic *204*

Pappardelle with Cherry Tomatoes, Rocket & Mozzarella *206*

Pasta with Roasted Vegetables & Toasted Almonds *208*

Creamy Ricotta, Mint & Garlic Pasta *210*

Creamy Pea & Watercress Pasta *212*

Fusilli with Courgettes & Lemon *214*

Vegetarian

Fresh Tomato Soup with Pasta

 SERVES 4    PREP TIME: 15 minutes   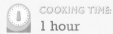 COOKING TIME: 1 hour

nutritional information per serving	135 kcals, 3.5g fat, 0.6g saturated fat, 6g sugar, 0.4g salt

Tomatoes are our major source of dietary lycopene, a carotene antioxidant that fights heart disease and may help prevent prostate cancer. They also contain vitamin C, quercetin and lutein.

INGREDIENTS

1 tbsp olive oil
4 large plum tomatoes
1 onion, cut into quarters
1 garlic clove, thinly sliced
1 celery stick, roughly chopped
500 ml/18 fl oz vegetable stock
55 g/2 oz dried soup pasta
salt and pepper
chopped fresh flat-leaf parsley, to garnish

1. Pour the oil into a large heavy-based saucepan and add the tomatoes, onion, garlic and celery. Cover and cook over a low heat, occasionally shaking gently, for 45 minutes, until pulpy.

2. Transfer the mixture to a food processor or blender and process to a smooth purée.

3. Push the purée through a sieve into a clean saucepan.

4. Add the stock and bring to the boil. Add the pasta, bring back to the boil and cook for 8–10 minutes, until the pasta is tender but still firm to the bite. Season to taste with salt and pepper. Ladle into warmed bowls, garnish with parsley and serve immediately.

1

3

4

VARIATION:
Replace the chopped
fresh parsley with
the same amount of
chopped fresh chives
and serve with
freshly grated
Parmesan cheese
sprinkled on the top.

Hearty Bean & Pasta Soup

 SERVES 4    PREP TIME: 10 minutes   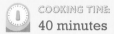 COOKING TIME: 40 minutes

nutritional information per serving	456 kcals, 16g fat, 4g saturated fat, 8g sugar, 1.3g salt

Add a little Tuscan sunshine to your dinner table with this colourful and satisfying traditional soup.

INGREDIENTS

4 tbsp olive oil

1 onion, finely chopped

1 celery stick, finely chopped

1 carrot, diced

1 bay leaf

1.2 litres/2 pints vegetable stock

400 g/14 oz canned chopped tomatoes

175 g/6 oz dried farfalle

400 g/14 oz canned cannellini beans, drained and rinsed

200 g/7 oz spinach or chard, thick stalks removed and shredded

salt and pepper

40 g/1½ oz Parmesan-style vegetarian cheese, finely grated, to serve

1. Heat the oil in a large, heavy-based saucepan. Add the onion, celery and carrot and cook over a medium heat for 10 minutes, stirring occasionally, until the vegetables slightly soften. Add the bay leaf, stock and tomatoes, then bring to the boil.

2. Reduce the heat, cover and simmer for 15 minutes, or until the vegetables are just tender. Add the pasta and beans, bring back to the boil and cook for 8–10 minutes, until the pasta is tender but still firm to the bite.

3. Stir occasionally to prevent the pasta sticking to the bottom of the pan and burning. Season to taste with salt and pepper, add the spinach and cook for a further 2 minutes, or until tender. Remove and discard the bay leaf. Ladle the soup into warmed bowls and serve immediately with grated Parmesan cheese.

Potato & Pasta Soup with Pesto

 SERVES 4    PREP TIME: 15 minutes    COOKING TIME: 45 minutes

nutritional information per serving	985 kcals, 73.6g fat, 24.1g sat fat, 15.7g total sugars, 0.9g salt

The simplest of fresh ingredients are combined to make this appetizing meal-in-a-bowl soup.

INGREDIENTS

450 g/1 lb floury potatoes, peeled and finely chopped

450 g/1 lb onions, finely chopped

600 ml/1 pint vegetable stock

600 ml/1 pint milk

100 g/3½ oz dried conchigliette

150 ml/5 fl oz double cream

2 tbsp chopped fresh flat-leaf parsley

salt and pepper

Parmesan-style vegetarian cheese shavings, to serve

parsley pesto

55 g/2 oz fresh flat-leaf parsley leaves

2 garlic cloves, chopped

55 g/2 oz pine kernels

2 tbsp chopped fresh basil leaves

55 g/2 oz Parmesan-style vegetarian cheese, grated

150 ml/5 fl oz olive oil

1. To make the pesto, put all of the ingredients in a food processor or blender and process for 2 minutes, or blend by hand using a mortar and pestle.

2. Place a large saucepan over medium heat. Add the potatoes and onion and cook, stirring constantly, for 12 minutes.

3. Add the stock and milk to the pan, bring to the boil and simmer for 10 minutes. Add the pasta, bring back to the boil and cook for 8–10 minutes, until tender but still firm to the bite.

4. Stir in the cream and simmer for 5 minutes. Add the chopped parsley and 2 tablespoons of the pesto. Season to taste with salt and pepper. Ladle the soup into serving bowls and serve immediately with the Parmesan-style vegetarian cheese shavings.

Tomato, Olive & Mozzarella Pasta Salad

 SERVES 4

 PREP TIME:
5 minutes

 COOKING TIME:
15 minutes

nutritional information per serving	385 kcals, 36g fat, 10g sat fat, 8g total sugars, 0.7g salt

When you taste this classic combination of ingredients, you'll know why it is so popular in Italy.

INGREDIENTS

225 g/8 oz dried conchiglie

50 g/1¾ oz pine kernels

350 g/12 oz cherry tomatoes, halved

1 red pepper, deseeded and cut into bite-size chunks

1 red onion, chopped

200 g/7 oz mozzarella di bufala, cut into small pieces

12 black olives, stoned

25 g/1 oz fresh basil leaves

Parmesan-style vegetarian cheese shavings, to garnish

salt

dressing

5 tbsp extra virgin olive oil

2 tbsp balsamic vinegar

1 tbsp chopped fresh basil

salt and pepper

1. Bring a large saucepan of lightly salted water to the boil. Add the pasta, bring back to the boil and cook for 8–10 minutes, until tender but still firm to the bite. Drain thoroughly and leave to cool.

2. Meanwhile, heat a dry frying pan over a low heat, add the pine kernels, and cook, shaking the pan frequently, for 1–2 minutes until lightly toasted. Remove from the heat, transfer to a dish and leave to cool.

3. To make the dressing, put all the ingredients in a small bowl and mix together well. Cover with clingfilm and set aside.

4. Divide the pasta among four serving bowls. Add the pine kernels, tomatoes, pepper, onion, mozzarella and olives to each bowl. Sprinkle over the basil, then drizzle over the dressing. Garnish with Parmesan-style vegetarian cheese shavings and serve.

Chilli Broccoli Pasta

 SERVES 4

 PREP TIME:
5 minutes

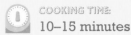 COOKING TIME:
10–15 minutes

nutritional information per serving	300 kcals, 11g fat, 1.5g sat fat, 3g total sugars, trace salt

A dish made with these ingredients can't fail – they just seem right together. Good for serving to a crowd.

INGREDIENTS

225 g/8 oz dried penne or macaroni

225 g/8 oz head of broccoli, cut into florets

50 ml/2 fl oz extra virgin olive oil

2 large garlic cloves, chopped

2 fresh red chillies, deseeded and diced

8 cherry tomatoes

handful of fresh basil leaves, to garnish

salt

1. Bring a large saucepan of lightly salted water to the boil. Add the pasta, return to the boil and cook for 8–10 minutes, until tender but still firm to the bite. Drain the pasta, refresh under cold running water and drain again. Set aside.

2. Bring a separate saucepan of lightly salted water to the boil, add the broccoli and cook for 5 minutes. Drain, refresh under cold running water and drain again.

3. Heat the oil in a large, heavy-based frying pan over high heat. Add the garlic, chillies and tomatoes and cook, stirring constantly, for 1 minute.

4. Add the broccoli and mix well. Cook for 2 minutes, stirring, to heat through. Add the pasta and mix well again. Cook for a further minute. Transfer the pasta to a large, warmed serving bowl and serve immediately, garnished with basil leaves.

1

2

4

COOK'S NOTE
Don't be tempted to chop fresh basil with a knife - it just turns black. Use small leaves or tear larger ones into pieces.

Double Cheese Macaroni

 SERVES 4

 PREP TIME:
10 minutes

 COOKING TIME:
15 minutes

nutritional information
per serving | 1109 kcals, 66g fat, 24g sat fat, 9g total sugars, 3g salt

This is an especially rich and tasty variation of a family favourite, equally popular with children and adults.

INGREDIENTS

225 g/8 oz dried macaroni

250 g/9 oz ricotta-style vegetarian cheese

1½ tbsp wholegrain mustard

3 tbsp snipped fresh chives, plus extra to garnish

200 g/7 oz cherry tomatoes, halved

100 g/3½ oz sun-dried tomatoes in oil, drained and chopped

butter or oil, for greasing

100 g/3½ oz vegetarian Cheddar cheese, grated

salt and pepper

1. Preheat the grill to high. Bring a large saucepan of lightly salted water to the boil. Add the pasta, bring back to the boil and cook for 8–10 minutes, until tender but still firm to the bite. Drain.

2. In a large bowl, mix the ricotta-style vegetarian cheese with the mustard and chives and season to taste with salt and pepper.

3. Stir in the macaroni, cherry tomatoes and sun-dried tomatoes and mix well.

4. Grease a 1.7-litre/3-pint shallow ovenproof dish. Spoon in the macaroni mixture, spreading evenly.

5. Sprinkle the Cheddar cheese over the macaroni mixture and cook under the preheated grill for 4–5 minutes, until golden and bubbling. Serve the macaroni immediately sprinkled with extra chives.

Penne with Asparagus & Blue Cheese

 SERVES 4

 PREP TIME:
10 minutes

 COOKING TIME:
25 minutes

nutritional information
per serving | 805 kcals, 48g fat, 28g saturated fat, 5g sugar, 1.1g salt

It's hard to believe that a dish so stunning is also so simple and requires almost no effort to prepare.

INGREDIENTS

450 g/1 lb asparagus spears

1 tbsp olive oil

225 g/8 oz vegetarian blue cheese, crumbled

175 ml/6 fl oz double cream

350 g/12 oz dried penne

salt and pepper

1. Preheat the oven to 230°C/450°F/Gas Mark 8. Place the asparagus spears in a single layer in a shallow ovenproof dish. Sprinkle with the oil and season to taste with salt and pepper. Turn to coat in the oil and seasoning. Roast in the preheated oven for 10–12 minutes until slightly browned and just tender. Set aside and keep warm.

2. Combine the cheese with the cream in a bowl. Season to taste with salt and pepper.

3. Bring a large saucepan of lightly salted water to the boil. Add the pasta, bring back to the boil and cook for 8–10 minutes, until tender but still firm to the bite. Drain and transfer to a warmed serving dish. Immediately add the asparagus and the cheese mixture. Toss well until the cheese has melted and the pasta is coated with the sauce. Serve immediately.

1

2

3

GOES WELL WITH
Freshly baked sourdough bread would be just the thing for mopping up every last bit of this lovely creamy sauce.

Rigatoni with Peppers & Goat's Cheese

 SERVES 4

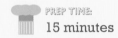 PREP TIME: 15 minutes

 COOKING TIME: 35 minutes

nutritional information per serving	637 kcals, 21g fat, 9g saturated fat, 13g sugar, 0.7g salt

Tangy cheese, slightly sharp peppers and succulent olives are combined in a rich and pungent sauce.

INGREDIENTS

2 tbsp olive oil

1 tbsp butter

1 small onion, finely chopped

4 red peppers, deseeded and cut into 2-cm/¾-inch squares

3 garlic cloves, thinly sliced

450 g/1 lb dried rigatoni

125 g/4½ oz goat's cheese, crumbled

15 fresh basil leaves, shredded

10 black olives, stoned and sliced

salt and pepper

1. Heat the oil and butter in a large frying pan over a medium heat. Add the onion and cook until soft. Increase the heat to medium–high and add the peppers and garlic. Cook for 12–15 minutes, stirring, until the peppers are tender but not mushy. Season to taste with salt and pepper. Remove from the heat.

2. Bring a large saucepan of lightly salted water to the boil. Add the pasta, bring back to the boil and cook for 8–10 minutes, or until tender but still firm to the bite. Drain and transfer to a warmed serving dish. Add the goat's cheese and toss to mix.

3. Briefly reheat the sauce. Add the basil and olives. Pour over the pasta and toss well to mix. Serve immediately.

GOES WELL WITH
A salad of peppery
leaves, such as rocket,
radicchio and watercress
contrasts deliciously
with this gorgeous dish.

Pasta with Camembert

nutritional information per serving	722 kcals, 46g fat, 28g sat fat, 2g total sugars, 0.9g salt

This rich and creamy dish looks especially appetizing if you use green pasta to contrast with the light sauce.

INGREDIENTS

55 g/2 oz unsalted butter

225 g/8 oz Camembert-style vegetarian cheese, rind removed, diced

150 ml/5 fl oz double cream

2 tbsp dry white wine

1 tsp cornflour

1 tbsp chopped chervil

300 g/10½ oz dried tagliatelle or fettuccine

salt

green salad, to serve

1. Melt half the butter in a heavy-based saucepan. Add 175 g/6 oz of the cheese and cook over a very low heat for about 2 minutes until melted.

2. Whisk in the cream, wine and cornflour and stir in the chervil. Cook, whisking constantly, until thickened and smooth, then remove from the heat.

3. Bring a large saucepan of lightly salted water to the boil. Add the pasta, bring back to the boil and cook for 8–10 minutes, until tender but still firm to the bite. Drain, return to the pan and toss with the remaining butter.

4. Return the pan of cheese sauce to a low heat and reheat gently, whisking constantly. Divide the pasta between warmed plates. Spoon the cheese sauce over it, sprinkle with the remaining cheese and serve immediately with a green salad.

SOMETHING
DIFFERENT
For a sauce with
a more powerful,
but still subtle
flavour, use a
vegetarian blue
cheese.

Creamy Asparagus & Brie Tagliatelle

 SERVES 4

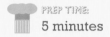 PREP TIME:
5 minutes

 COOKING TIME:
10–15 minutes

nutritional information
per serving : 634 kcals, 31g fat, 18g sat fat, 4g total sugars, 0.8g salt

This is truly a special occasion dish and is sure to impress your guests – you don't have to tell them how quick and easy it is!

INGREDIENTS

350 g/12 oz dried tagliatelle
25 g/1 oz butter
1 tbsp olive oil
225 g/8 oz asparagus spears
1 garlic clove, finely chopped
1 tbsp chopped fresh thyme
150 ml/5 fl oz single cream
200 g/7 oz Brie-style vegetarian cheese, diced
salt

1. Bring a large saucepan of lightly salted water to the boil. Add the pasta, bring back to the boil and cook for 8–10 minutes, until tender but still firm to the bite.

2. Meanwhile, melt the butter with the oil in a frying pan, add the asparagus spears and cook over a low heat, stirring occasionally, for 3 minutes. Add the garlic and cook, stirring frequently, for a further 2 minutes. Stir in the thyme and cream, increase the heat to medium and bring just to the boil, stirring constantly. Stir in the cheese and remove the pan from the heat.

3. Drain the pasta and tip it into the pan of sauce. Toss gently until the cheese is just melted and the sauce is creamy. Transfer to warmed plates and serve immediately.

COOK'S NOTE
The Brie must
be ripe and soft
but certainly not
runny.

Linguine with Lemon, Chilli & Spinach

 SERVES 4   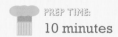 PREP TIME: 10 minutes    COOKING TIME: 25 minutes

nutritional information per serving	540 kcals, 21g fat, 8g sat fat, 4g total sugars, 0.7g salt

The lovely, light summery flavours make this a perfect dish for an al fresco meal and it's great for easy entertaining.

INGREDIENTS

350 g/12 oz dried linguine

2 tbsp olive oil, plus extra for drizzling

2 garlic cloves, finely chopped

1 red chilli, deseeded (optional) and finely chopped

finely grated rind and juice of 1 lemon

225 g/8 oz ricotta cheese

280 g/10 oz baby spinach, coarse stalks removed

4 tbsp freshly grated Parmesan-style vegetarian cheese

salt and pepper

1. Bring a large saucepan of lightly salted water to the boil. Add the pasta, bring back to the boil and cook for 8–10 minutes, until tender but still firm to the bite. Drain, reserving 6 tablespoons of the cooking liquid, then return to the pan. Drizzle with a little oil, toss gently and set aside.

2. Heat the oil in another saucepan, add the garlic and chilli and cook over a low heat, stirring frequently, for 2 minutes. Stir in the lemon rind and juice, ricotta cheese and reserved cooking liquid. Season to taste with salt and pepper and bring to simmering point, stirring frequently.

3. Add the spinach, in two to three batches, and cook for 2–3 minutes until wilted. Taste and adjust the seasoning, if necessary, then tip the sauce into the pan of pasta. Toss well, then divide between warmed plates. Sprinkle with the Parmesan-style vegetarian cheese and serve immediately.

COOK'S NOTE
If you warm the lemon on high in the microwave for a few seconds, it will yield more juice when you squeeze it.

Spaghetti Olio E Aglio

 SERVES 4

 PREP TIME:
5 minutes

 COOKING TIME:
15 minutes

nutritional information
per serving

590 kcals, 25g fat, 3.5g saturated fat, 3.5g sugar, trace salt

An inexpensive dish created by the poor, this Roman classic is now popular throughout Italy.

INGREDIENTS

450 g/1 lb dried spaghetti

125 ml/4 fl oz extra virgin olive oil

3 garlic cloves, finely chopped

3 tbsp chopped fresh flat-leaf parsley

salt and pepper

1. Bring a large saucepan of lightly salted water to the boil. Add the pasta, bring back to the boil and cook for 8–10 minutes, until tender but still firm to the bite.

2. Meanwhile, heat the oil in a heavy-based frying pan. Add the garlic and a pinch of salt and cook over a low heat, stirring constantly, for 3–4 minutes, or until golden. Do not allow the garlic to brown or it will taste bitter. Remove the frying pan from the heat.

3. Drain the pasta and transfer to a warmed serving dish. Pour in the garlic-flavoured oil, then add the chopped parsley and season to taste with salt and pepper. Toss well and serve immediately.

TO SERVE

Cooked pasta gets cold quickly, so make sure to transfer to a warmed serving plate once drained.

Pasta with Leek & Butternut Squash

 SERVES 4

 PREP TIME:
15 minutes

 COOKING TIME:
40 minutes

nutritional information per serving	334 kcals, 5g fat, 1.5g saturated fat, 9g sugar, 0.4g salt

This unusual dish combines the sweetness of roasted vegetables with warm spice and aromatic coriander.

INGREDIENTS

150 g/5½ oz baby leeks, cut into 2-cm/¾ -inch slices

175 g/6 oz butternut squash, deseeded and cut into 2-cm/¾ -inch chunks

1½ tbsp medium curry paste

1 tsp vegetable oil

175 g/6 oz cherry tomatoes

250 g/9 oz dried farfalle

2 tbsp chopped fresh coriander

salt

white sauce

250 ml/9 fl oz skimmed milk

20 g/¾ oz cornflour

1 tsp mustard powder

1 small onion, left whole

2 small bay leaves

4 tsp grated Parmesan-style vegetarian cheese

1. To make the white sauce, put the milk into a saucepan with the cornflour, mustard powder, onion and bay leaves. Whisk over a medium heat until thick. Remove from the heat, discard the onion and bay leaves and stir in the cheese. Set aside, stirring occasionally to prevent a skin forming. Preheat the oven to 200°C/400°F/Gas Mark 6.

2. Bring a large saucepan of water to the boil, add the leeks and cook for 2 minutes. Add the butternut squash and cook for a further 2 minutes. Drain in a colander. Mix the curry paste with the oil in a large bowl. Toss the leeks and butternut squash in the mixture to coat thoroughly.

3. Transfer the leeks and squash to a non-stick baking sheet and roast in the preheated oven for 10 minutes until golden brown. Add the tomatoes and roast for a further 5 minutes.

4. Meanwhile, bring a large saucepan of lightly salted water to the boil. Add the pasta, bring back to the boil and cook for 8–10 minutes, until tender but still firm to the bite. Drain well. Put the white sauce into a large saucepan and warm over a low heat. Add the leeks, squash, tomatoes and coriander and stir in the pasta. Transfer to warmed plates and serve immediately.

Conchiglie with Marinated Artichoke

 SERVES 4

 PREP TIME:
10 minutes

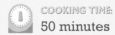 COOKING TIME:
50 minutes

nutritional information per serving	500 kcals, 19g fat, 3.5g saturated fat, 7g sugar, 1.4g salt

This would be an excellent choice for an unusual first course for a formal dinner party.

INGREDIENTS

280 g/10 oz marinated artichoke hearts from a jar

3 tbsp olive oil

1 onion, finely chopped

3 garlic cloves, crushed

1 tsp dried oregano

½ tsp dried chilli flakes

400 g/14 oz canned chopped tomatoes

350 g/12 oz dried conchiglie

4 tsp freshly grated Parmesan-style vegetarian cheese

3 tbsp chopped fresh flat-leaf parsley

salt and pepper

1. Drain the artichoke hearts, reserving the marinade. Heat the oil in a large, deep frying pan over a medium heat. Add the onion and fry for 5 minutes until translucent. Add the garlic, oregano, chilli flakes and the reserved artichoke marinade. Cook for a further 5 minutes.

2. Stir in the tomatoes. Bring to the boil, then simmer over a medium-low heat for 30 minutes. Season to taste with salt and pepper.

3. Bring a large saucepan of lightly salted water to the boil. Add the pasta, bring back to the boil and cook for 8–10 minutes, until tender but still firm to the bite. Drain and transfer to a warmed serving dish.

4. Cut the artichokes into quarters and add to the sauce with the Parmesan-style vegetarian cheese and parsley. Cook for a few minutes until heated through. Pour the sauce over the pasta, toss well to mix and serve immediately.

Spicy Aubergine, Chickpea & Coriander Penne

 SERVES 4    PREP TIME: 15 minutes    COOKING TIME: 45 minutes

nutritional information per serving	444 kcals, 9g fat, 1g saturated fat, 10g sugar, 0.8g salt

Pasta with more than a hint of North African cuisine makes a wonderfully warming and unusual dish.

INGREDIENTS

large pinch of saffron threads

450 ml/16 fl oz hot vegetable stock

2 tbsp olive oil

1 large onion, roughly chopped

1 tsp cumin seeds, crushed

350 g/12 oz aubergine, diced

1 large red pepper, deseeded and chopped

400 g/14 oz canned chopped tomatoes with garlic

1 tsp ground cinnamon

30 g/1 oz fresh coriander, leaves and stalks separated and roughly chopped

400 g/14 oz canned chickpeas, drained and rinsed

280 g/10 oz dried penne

salt and pepper

harissa or chilli sauce, to serve (optional)

1. Toast the saffron threads in a dry frying pan set over a medium heat for 20–30 seconds, just until they begin to give off their aroma. Place in a small bowl and crumble with your fingers. Add 2 tablespoons of the hot stock and set aside to infuse.

2. Heat the oil in a large saucepan. Add the onion and fry for 5–6 minutes, until golden brown. Add the cumin seeds and fry for a further 20-30 seconds.

3. Stir in the aubergine, red pepper, tomatoes, cinnamon, coriander stalks, saffron liquid and remaining stock. Cover and simmer for 20 minutes.

4. Add the chickpeas to the pan and season to taste with salt and pepper. Simmer for a further 5 minutes, removing the lid to reduce and thicken the sauce if necessary.

5. Bring a large saucepan of lightly salted water to the boil. Add the pasta, bring back to the boil and cook for 8–10 minutes, until tender but still firm to the bite. Drain and transfer to a warmed serving bowl. Add the sauce and half the coriander leaves, then toss. Garnish with the remaining coriander and serve immediately with harissa or chilli sauce, if desired.

Ziti with Rocket

 SERVES 4

 PREP TIME:
20 minutes
plus resting

 COOKING TIME:
20 minutes

nutritional information
per serving   435 kcals, 16g fat, 2g sat fat, 2.5g total sugars, trace salt

This pungent dish from Puglia in the 'heel' of Italy looks and tastes absolutely delicious.

INGREDIENTS

2 fresh red chillies, thinly sliced, plus 4 whole chillies to garnish

350 g/12 oz dried ziti, broken into 4-cm/1½-inch lengths

5 tbsp extra virgin olive oil

2 garlic cloves, left whole

200 g/7 oz rocket

Parmesan-style vegetarian cheese, grated

1. For the red chilli garnish, use a sharp knife to remove the tip and cut the chilli lengthways, almost to the stem. Deseed and repeat the cutting process to create 'petals' of an equal length. Place the flowers in a bowl of iced water for 15-20 minutes to encourage the petals to fan out.

2. Bring a large saucepan of lightly salted water to the boil. Add the pasta, bring back to the boil and cook for 8–10 minutes, until tender but still firm to the bite.

3. Meanwhile, heat the oil in a large, heavy-based frying pan. Add the garlic, rocket and sliced chillies and fry for 5 minutes, or until the rocket has wilted.

4. Stir 2 tablespoons of the pasta cooking water into the rocket, then drain the pasta and add to the frying pan. Cook, stirring frequently, for 2 minutes, then transfer to a warmed serving dish. Remove and discard the garlic cloves and sliced chillies, garnish with red chilli flowers and serve immediately with the Parmesan cheese.

1

3

4

GOES WELL WITH
This would be good with plum tomatoes roasted with garlic, dressed with olive oil and balsamic vinegar and served warm or cold.

Garlic Mushroom Pasta

 SERVES 4

 PREP TIME: 15 minutes

 COOKING TIME: 25 minutes

nutritional information
per serving | 804 kcals, 51g fat, 25g saturated fat, 4g sugar, 0.6g salt

The perfect choice for a midweek supper, this speedy dish is full of flavour but requires very little effort to prepare.

INGREDIENTS

400 g/14 oz dried spaghetti

4 tbsp olive oil

650 g/1 lb 7 oz oyster mushrooms, torn into large pieces

3 garlic cloves, finely chopped

55 g/2 oz butter

1 tsp chopped fresh thyme

1 tbsp chopped fresh flat-leaf parsley

200 ml/7 fl oz double cream

salt and pepper

grated Parmesan-style vegetarian cheese, to serve

1. Bring a large saucepan of lightly salted water to the boil. Add the pasta, bring back to the boil and cook for 8–10 minutes, until tender but still firm to the bite.

2. Meanwhile, heat the oil in a large frying pan, add the mushrooms and cook over a high heat, stirring occasionally, for 3–4 minutes, until lightly browned. Reduce the heat, add the garlic and cook, stirring occasionally, for a further 6–8 minutes.

3. Drain the pasta and return it to the pan. Add the butter, season to taste with pepper and toss well.

4. Stir the thyme and parsley into the pan of mushrooms, season to taste with salt and pepper and stir in the cream. Remove the pan from the heat. Tip the pasta into a warmed serving dish, top with the mushroom mixture and serve immediately, with the cheese separately.

HEALTHY HINT
Low-fat cream has about half the fat content of double cream and crème fraîche has about two-thirds. Both work well in this recipe.

Linguine with Wild Mushrooms

 SERVES 4

 PREP TIME:
10 minutes

 COOKING TIME:
30 minutes

nutritional information
per serving

773 kcals, 48g fat, 31g saturated fat, 5g sugar, 0.6g salt

The flavour of wild mushrooms is incomparable and goes superbly with garlic, basil and cheese.

INGREDIENTS

55 g/2 oz butter

1 onion, chopped

1 garlic clove, finely chopped

350 g/12 oz wild mushrooms, sliced

350 g/12 oz dried linguine

300 ml/10 fl oz crème fraîche

2 tbsp shredded fresh basil leaves, plus extra to garnish

4 tbsp grated Parmesan-style vegetarian cheese, plus extra to serve

salt and pepper

1. Melt the butter in a large heavy-based frying pan. Add the onion and garlic and cook over a low heat for 5 minutes, or until softened. Add the mushrooms and cook, stirring occasionally, for a further 10 minutes.

2. Meanwhile, bring a large saucepan of lightly salted water to the boil. Add the pasta, bring back to the boil and cook for 8–10 minutes, until tender but still firm to the bite.

3. Stir the crème fraîche, basil and cheese into the mushroom mixture and season to taste with salt and pepper. Cover and heat through gently for 1–2 minutes. Drain the pasta and transfer to a warmed serving dish. Add the mushroom mixture and toss lightly. Garnish with extra basil and serve immediately with extra cheese.

1

2

3

GOES WELL WITH
The sweetness
of a tomato and
red onion salad
would balance
the earthiness of
wild mushrooms
beautifully.

Macaroni with Chickpeas, Herbs & Garlic

 SERVES 4

 PREP TIME:
5 minutes

 COOKING TIME:
20 minutes

nutritional information
per serving
464 kcals, 12g fat, 1.5g sat fat, 3.5g total sugars, 0.4g salt

A filling and warming dish, this will satisfy even the heartiest appetite on a chilly winter evening.

INGREDIENTS

350 g/12 oz dried macaroni

3 tbsp olive oil

1 onion, finely chopped

1 garlic clove, crushed

400 g/14 oz canned chickpeas, drained

4 tbsp passata

2 tbsp chopped fresh oregano

small handful of basil leaves, shredded, plus extra sprigs to garnish

salt and pepper

1. Bring a large saucepan of lightly salted water to the boil. Add the pasta, bring back to the boil and cook for 8–10 minutes, until tender but still firm to the bite. Drain thoroughly.

2. Meanwhile, heat the oil in a saucepan and fry the onion and garlic, stirring occasionally, for 4–5 minutes, until golden.

3. Add the chickpeas and passata to the pan and stir until heated through.

4. Stir the pasta into the pan with the oregano and shredded basil. Season to taste with salt and pepper and serve immediately, garnished with a sprig of basil.

1

3

4

GOES WELL WITH
The slightly chewy
texture and savoury
aroma of rosemary
or onion focaccia would
be just right with
this dish.

Pappardelle with Cherry Tomatoes, Rocket & Mozzarella

 SERVES 4

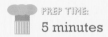 PREP TIME:
5 minutes

 COOKING TIME:
20 minutes

nutritional information per serving	1218 kcals, 46g fat, 23g saturated fat, 10g sugar, 1.6g salt

Creamy cheese, pungent leaves and sweet tomatoes are a great combination that tastes as good as it looks.

INGREDIENTS

400 g/14 oz dried pappardelle

2 tbsp olive oil

1 garlic clove, chopped

350 g/12 oz cherry tomatoes, halved

85 g/3 oz rocket leaves

300 g/10½ oz mozzarella, chopped

salt and pepper

grated Parmesan-style vegetarian cheese, to serve

1. Bring a large saucepan of lightly salted water to the boil. Add the pasta, bring back to the boil and cook for 8–10 minutes, until tender but still firm to the bite.

2. Meanwhile, heat the oil in a frying pan over a medium heat and fry the garlic, stirring, for 1 minute, without browning.

3. Add the tomatoes, season well with salt and pepper and cook gently for 2–3 minutes, until softened.

4. Drain the pasta and stir into the frying pan. Add the rocket leaves and mozzarella, then stir until the leaves wilt.

5. Serve the pasta in warmed dishes, sprinkled with the Parmesan-style vegetarian cheese.

1

3

4

GOES WELL WITH
While not a traditional
Italian accompaniment,
rye bread would be
a good choice to serve
with this flavoursome
dish.

Pasta with Roasted Vegetables & Toasted Almonds

 SERVES 4

 PREP TIME: 20 minutes

 COOKING TIME: 1 hour

nutritional information **per serving** | 542 kcals, 23g fat, 3g saturated fat, 10g sugar, trace salt

With its attractive appearance and appetizing aroma this colourful dish is guaranteed to become a firm family favourite.

INGREDIENTS

1 aubergine, coarsely diced

1 red pepper, deseeded and diced

1 yellow pepper, deseeded and diced

2 courgettes, coarsely diced

6 tbsp olive oil

2 tbsp chopped fresh parsley

225 g/8 oz cherry tomatoes, halved

2 garlic cloves, finely chopped

350 g/12 oz dried rigatoni

25 g/1 oz flaked almonds

salt and pepper

1. Preheat the oven to 180°C/350°F/Gas Mark 4. Put the aubergine, red pepper, yellow pepper and courgettes into a roasting tin. Drizzle with half the oil, sprinkle with the parsley and season to taste with salt and pepper. Roast in the preheated oven for 30 minutes. Remove the tin from the oven, add the tomatoes and garlic, toss well and return to the oven. Roast for a further 30 minutes.

2. Shortly before the vegetables are ready, bring a large saucepan of lightly salted water to the boil. Add the pasta, bring back to the boil and cook for 8–10 minutes, until tender but still firm to the bite.

3. Meanwhile, heat 1 tablespoon of the remaining oil in a small frying pan, add the almonds and cook over a low heat, shaking the pan frequently, for 2–3 minutes until the almonds are golden. Tip out onto kitchen paper to drain.

4. Drain the pasta and tip it into a warmed serving dish. Add the roasted vegetables, drizzle with the remaining oil and toss. Garnish with the toasted almonds and serve immediately.

SOMETHING
DIFFERENT
This dish is also
excellent served
cold. Leave the
pasta and
vegetables to cool
before garnishing
with the almonds.

Creamy Ricotta, Mint & Garlic Pasta

 SERVES 4

 PREP TIME:
5 minutes

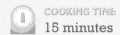 COOKING TIME:
15 minutes

nutritional information per serving	500 kcals, 25g fat, 15g sat fat, 3g total sugars, 0.1g salt

This is a fabulous choice for a summery meal when you want to minimize the time spent in the kitchen.

INGREDIENTS

300 g/10½ oz dried fusilli

140 g/5 oz ricotta-style vegetarian cheese

1–2 roasted garlic cloves from a jar, finely chopped

150 ml/5 fl oz double cream

1 tbsp chopped fresh mint, plus extra sprigs to garnish

salt and pepper

fresh crusty bread, to serve

1. Bring a large saucepan of lightly salted water to the boil. Add the pasta, bring back to the boil and cook for 8–10 minutes, until tender but still firm to the bite.

2. Beat together the ricotta, garlic, cream and chopped mint in a bowl until smooth.

3. Drain the pasta then tip back into the pan. Pour in the cheese mixture and toss together.

4. Season with pepper and serve immediately with fresh crusty bread, garnished with fresh mint.

GOES WELL WITH
A light cucumber
and watermelon
salad would be
a cooling and
refreshing
accompaniment to
this creamy dish.

Creamy Pea & Watercress Pasta

 SERVES 4

 PREP TIME:
20 minutes

 COOKING TIME:
30 minutes

nutritional information per serving	434 kcals, 6.5g fat, 2g saturated fat, 4g sugar, 0.4g salt

The peppery sharpness of watercress goes beautifully with the sweetness of fresh young peas in this lovely summery dish.

INGREDIENTS

1 tbsp olive oil

1 garlic clove, finely chopped

2 shallots, finely chopped

300 g/10½ oz shelled peas

2 tbsp chopped sage

450 ml/16 fl oz vegetable stock

350 g/12 oz dried penne

100 g/3½ oz fresh watercress, coarse stalks removed

finely grated rind and juice of 1 lemon

2 tbsp Greek-style yogurt

salt and white pepper

fresh crusty bread, to serve

1. Heat the oil in a saucepan, add the garlic and shallots and cook over a low heat, stirring occasionally, for 4–5 minutes until soft. Add the peas, sage and stock, increase the heat to medium and bring to the boil. Reduce the heat and simmer for 10–15 minutes until the peas are tender.

2. Meanwhile, bring a large saucepan of lightly salted water to the boil. Add the pasta, bring back to the boil and cook for 8–10 minutes, until tender but still firm to the bite. Drain and return to the pan.

3. Drain the vegetables, reserving 2 tablespoons of the stock. Put the vegetables, reserved stock and watercress into a food processor or blender and process briefly to a coarse purée. Scrape the purée into the pan of pasta, add the lemon rind and juice and yogurt, season to taste with salt and pepper and toss well. Transfer to warmed bowls and serve immediately with the fresh crusty bread.

COOK'S NOTE
For extra flavour, add
some of the (rinsed)
pea pods to the pan
when cooking the peas,
but remove them before
processing.

Fusilli with Courgettes & Lemon

 SERVES 4

 PREP TIME:
10 minutes

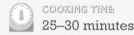 COOKING TIME:
25–30 minutes

nutritional information per serving	629 kcals, 23g fat, 6g sat fat, 6g total sugars, 0.3g salt

Deliciously fragrant, this light, summery dish would be a great choice for informal al fresco entertaining.

INGREDIENTS

6 tbsp olive oil

1 small onion, very thinly sliced

2 garlic cloves, very finely chopped

2 tbsp chopped fresh rosemary

1 tbsp chopped fresh flat-leaf parsley

450 g/1 lb small courgettes, cut into 4-cm/1½-inch strips

finely grated rind of 1 lemon

450 g/1 lb dried fusilli

salt and pepper

4 tbsp grated Parmesan-style vegetarian cheese, to serve

1. Heat the oil in a large frying pan over a low–medium heat. Add the onion and cook gently, stirring occasionally, for about 10 minutes, until golden.

2. Increase the heat to medium–high. Add the garlic, rosemary and parsley. Cook for a few seconds, stirring.

3. Add the courgettes and lemon rind. Cook for 5–7 minutes, stirring occasionally, until just tender. Season to taste with salt and pepper. Remove from the heat.

4. Bring a large saucepan of lightly salted water to the boil. Add the pasta, bring back to the boil and cook for 8–10 minutes, until tender but still firm to the bite.

5. Drain the pasta and transfer to a warmed serving dish. Briefly reheat the courgette sauce. Pour over the pasta and toss well to mix. Serve immediately with the Parmesan-style vegetarian cheese.

2

5

5

GOES WELL WITH

A salad of beansprouts, grapes and chopped nuts dressed with a nut oil vinaigrette would provide a delightful crunch factor.

Lasagne al Forno *218*

Warm Ravioli Salad *220*

Sicilian Spaghetti Cake *222*

Steak & Pasta Bites *224*

Pork & Pasta Bake *226*

Ham & Pesto Lasagne *228*

Chicken Ravioli in Tarragon Broth *230*

Chicken & Mushroom Lasagne *232*

Turkey & Mushroom Cannelloni *234*

Turkey Pasta Bake *236*

Turkey Manicotti *238*

Pasticcio *240*

Mixed Meat Lasagne *242*

Spinach & Tomato Tortellini Soup *244*

Parmesan-filled Tortellini Salad *246*

Spinach & Ricotta Cannelloni *248*

Pumpkin Ravioli *250*

Mushroom Cannelloni *252*

Broccoli & Mascarpone Cannelloni *254*

Spicy Vegetable Lasagne *256*

Tuna Pasta Bake *258*

Salmon Lasagne Rolls *260*

Layered Salmon & Prawn Spaghetti *262*

Macaroni & Seafood Bake *264*

Filled & Baked

Lasagne al Forno

 SERVES 6

 PREP TIME:
15 minutes

 COOKING TIME:
2¼ hours

nutritional information per serving	629 kcals, 71g fat, 30g saturated fat, 5g sugar, 2.8g salt

You need plenty of time to make a baked lasagne with an authentic flavour, but it is worth it.

INGREDIENTS

175 ml/6 fl oz olive oil

55 g/2 oz butter

100 g/3½ oz pancetta

1 onion, finely chopped

1 celery stick, finely chopped

1 carrot, finely chopped

350 g/12 oz braising steak, in a single piece

5 tbsp red wine

2 tbsp sun-dried tomato purée

200 g/7 oz Italian sausage

2 eggs

150 g/5½ oz freshly grated Parmesan cheese

30 g/1 oz fresh breadcrumbs

350 g/12 oz ricotta cheese

8 dried no pre-cook lasagne sheets

350 g/12 oz mozzarella cheese, sliced

salt and pepper

chopped fresh parsley, to garnish

1. Heat 125 ml/4 fl oz of the oil with the butter in a large saucepan. Add the pancetta, onion, celery and carrot and cook over a low heat, until soft. Increase the heat to medium, add the steak and cook until evenly browned. Stir in the wine and tomato purée, season with salt and pepper and bring to the boil. Reduce the heat, cover and simmer gently for 1½ hours, until the steak is tender.

2. Meanwhile, heat 2 tablespoons of the remaining oil in a frying pan. Add the sausage and cook for 8–10 minutes. Remove from the pan and discard the skin. Thinly slice the sausage and set aside. Transfer the steak to a chopping board and finely dice. Return half the steak to the sauce.

3. Mix the remaining steak in a bowl with 1 egg, 1 tablespoon of the Parmesan cheese and the breadcrumbs. Shape into walnut-sized balls. Heat the remaining oil in a frying pan, add the meatballs and cook for 5–8 minutes, until brown. Pass the ricotta through a sieve into a bowl. Stir in the remaining egg and 4 tablespoons of the remaining Parmesan cheese.

4. Preheat the oven to 180°C/350°F/Gas Mark 4. In a rectangular ovenproof dish, make layers with the lasagne sheets, ricotta mixture, meat sauce, meatballs, sausage and mozzarella cheese. Finish with a layer of the ricotta mixture and sprinkle with the remaining Parmesan cheese.

5. Bake the lasagne in the preheated oven for 20–25 minutes, until golden and bubbling. Serve immediately, garnished with chopped parsley.

Warm Ravioli Salad

 SERVES 4    PREP TIME: 20 minutes    COOKING TIME: 15 minutes

nutritional information per serving	748 kcals, 41g fat, 12g saturated fat, 12g sugar, 1.3g salt

This is a great dish for easy entertaining as it looks and tastes wonderful but requires very little effort.

INGREDIENTS

125 ml/4 fl oz olive oil

2 tbsp balsamic vinegar

1 tsp Dijon mustard

1 tsp sugar

½ small cucumber, peeled

225 g/8 oz mixed lettuce leaves

115 g/4 oz rocket

1 head chicory, sliced

3 tbsp mixed chopped herbs, such as parsley, thyme and coriander

2 tomatoes, cut into wedges

2 red peppers or yellow peppers preserved in oil, drained and sliced

20 fresh beef ravioli

25 g/1 oz butter

salt and pepper

1. Whisk 100 ml/3½ fl oz of the oil, the vinegar, mustard and sugar together in a bowl and season to taste with salt and pepper. Set aside.

2. Halve the cucumber lengthways and scoop out the seeds, then slice. Tear the lettuce and rocket leaves into small pieces. Put the cucumber, lettuce, rocket, chicory, herbs, tomatoes and preserved peppers into a bowl and set aside.

3. Bring a large saucepan of lightly salted water to the boil. Add the ravioli and cook according to the packet instructions, then drain. Melt the butter with the remaining oil in a frying pan. Add the ravioli and cook over a medium heat, turning carefully once or twice, for 5 minutes until golden on both sides. Remove the pan from the heat.

4. Pour the dressing over the salad and toss, then divide between individual serving plates. Top with the ravioli and serve immediately.

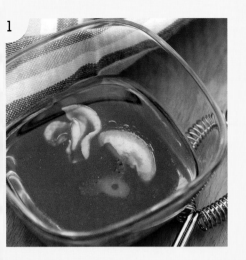

1

2

3

Sicilian Spaghetti Cake

 SERVES 4

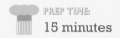 PREP TIME: 15 minutes

 COOKING TIME: 1¼ hours

nutritional information per serving	772 kcals, 51g fat, 17g saturated fat, 10.5g sugar, 1.1g salt

This delicious classic dish is perfect for both a family midweek supper or a special occasion main course.

INGREDIENTS

125 ml/4 fl oz olive oil, plus extra for greasing

2 aubergines, sliced

350 g/12 oz minced beef

1 onion, chopped

2 garlic cloves, chopped finely

2 tbsp tomato purée

400 g/14 oz canned chopped tomatoes

1 tsp Worcestershire sauce

1 tbsp chopped fresh flat-leaf parsley

10 stoned black olives, sliced

1 red pepper, deseeded and chopped

175 g/6 oz dried spaghetti

140 g/5 oz freshly grated Parmesan cheese

salt and pepper

1. Preheat the oven to 200°C/400°F/Gas Mark 6. Brush a 20-cm/ 8-inch loose-based round cake tin with oil and line the bottom with baking paper. Heat half the oil in a frying pan. Add the aubergines in batches, and cook until lightly browned on both sides. Add more oil, as required. Drain the aubergines on kitchen paper, then arrange in overlapping slices to cover the bottom and sides of the cake tin, reserving a few slices.

2. Heat the remaining oil in a large saucepan and add the beef, onion and garlic. Cook over a medium heat, breaking up the meat with a wooden spoon, until browned all over. Add the tomato purée, tomatoes and their can juices, Worcestershire sauce and parsley. Season to taste with salt and pepper and simmer for 10 minutes. Add the olives and red pepper and cook for 10 minutes.

3. Meanwhile, bring a large saucepan of lightly salted water to the boil. Add the pasta, bring back to the boil and cook for 8–10 minutes, until tender but still firm to the bite. Drain and transfer to a bowl. Add the meat sauce and cheese and toss, then spoon into the cake tin, press down and cover with the remaining aubergine slices. Bake for 40 minutes. Leave the cake to stand for 5 minutes, then loosen round the edges and invert onto a plate. Remove and discard the baking paper and serve immediately.

1

1

2

Steak & Pasta Bites

 SERVES 6

 PREP TIME: 25 minutes

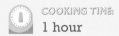 COOKING TIME: 1 hour

nutritional information per serving	800 kcals, 44g fat, 19g sat fat, 7g total sugars, 1.1g salt

This delicious deep-fried pasta treat rings the changes in the family menu and is a sure-fire hit with children.

INGREDIENTS

3 tbsp olive oil

2 onions, chopped

2 garlic cloves, finely chopped

400 g/14 oz canned chopped tomatoes

1 tsp soft light brown sugar

100 ml/3½ oz water

12–16 dried cannelloni tubes

450 g/1 lb fresh steak mince

1 tbsp chopped fresh flat-leaf parsley

pinch dried oregano

350 g/12 oz mozzarella cheese, grated

350 g/12 oz ricotta cheese

vegetable oil, for deep-frying

70 g/2½ oz plain flour

2 eggs, lightly beaten

85 g/3 oz fresh breadcrumbs

salt and pepper

1. Heat 2 tablespoons of the olive oil in a saucepan, add half the chopped onions and all the garlic and cook over a low heat for 5 minutes. Stir in the tomatoes, sugar and water and season to taste with salt and pepper. Simmer, stirring occasionally, for 20 minutes. Remove from the heat, ladle 125 ml/4 fl oz into a food processor or blender and process to a coarse purée. Set aside the remaining sauce.

2. Bring a saucepan of lightly salted water to the boil. Add the pasta, bring back to the boil and cook for 5–6 minutes. Drain and set aside on a tea towel.

3. Heat the remaining olive oil in a frying pan, add the remaining onion and cook over a low heat, stirring occasionally, for 5 minutes. Increase the heat to medium, add the mince and cook, stirring fquenly, for 5–7 minutes, until brown. Reduce the heat, stir in the herbs and puréed tomato sauce, season to taste with salt and pepper and simmer for 10 minutes. Remove from the heat and leave to cool.

4. Stir the mozzarella cheese and ricotta cheese into the meat mixture, then use to fill the cannelloni tubes. Chill in the freezer for 5 minutes. Heat the vegetable oil to 180–190°C/350–375°F or until a cube of day-old bread browns in 30 seconds. Cut each cannelloni tube into three pieces. Coat them in the flour, then in the beaten egg and, finally, in breadcrumbs. Add to the hot oil, in batches, and cook for 4–5 minutes, until crisp and golden. Remove and drain on kitchen paper. Reheat the reserved sauce, if necessary, and ladle onto warmed plates. Top with the pasta bites and serve immediately.

Pork & Pasta Bake

 SERVES 4   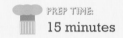 PREP TIME: 15 minutes   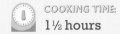 COOKING TIME: 1½ hours

nutritional information per serving	860 kcals, 46g fat, 23g saturated fat, 11g sugar, 1.6g salt

When cooking with olive oil, there is no need to use extra virgin olive oil as the flavour will be lost during cooking.

INGREDIENTS

2 tbsp olive oil

1 onion, chopped

1 garlic clove, finely chopped

2 carrots, diced

55 g/2 oz pancetta, chopped

115 g/4 oz mushrooms, chopped

450 g/1 lb minced pork

125 ml/4 fl oz dry white wine

4 tbsp passata

200 g/7 oz canned chopped tomatoes

2 tsp chopped fresh sage or ½ tsp dried sage

225 g/8 oz dried rigatoni

140 g/5 oz mozzarella cheese, diced

4 tbsp freshly grated Parmesan cheese

300 ml/10 fl oz hot Béchamel Sauce (see page 274)

salt and pepper

1. Preheat the oven to 200°C/400°F/Gas Mark 6. Heat the olive oil in a large, heavy-based frying pan. Add the onion, garlic and carrots and cook over a low heat, stirring occasionally, for 5 minutes, or until the onion has softened. Add the pancetta and cook for 5 minutes. Add the chopped mushrooms and cook, stirring occasionally, for an additional 2 minutes. Add the pork and cook, breaking it up with a wooden spoon, until the meat is browned all over. Stir in the wine, passata, chopped tomatoes and their can juices and sage. Season to taste with salt and pepper and bring to the boil, then cover and simmer over a low heat for 25–30 minutes.

2. Meanwhile, bring a large saucepan of lightly salted water to the boil. Add the pasta, bring back to the boil and cook for 8–10 minutes, until tender but still firm to the bite.

3. Spoon the pork mixture into a large ovenproof dish. Stir the mozzarella cheese and half the Parmesan cheese into the Béchamel Sauce. Drain the pasta and stir the sauce into it, then spoon it over the pork mixture. Sprinkle with the remaining Parmesan cheese and bake in the preheated oven for 25–30 minutes, until golden and bubbling. Serve immediately.

Ham & Pesto Lasagne

 SERVES 4–6

 PREP TIME:
20 minutes

 COOKING TIME:
1¼ hours

nutritional information **per serving**	545 kcals, 29g fat, 13g saturated fat, 7g sugar, 2g salt

While still rich and satisfying, this is a lighter-tasting dish than the more usual lasagne made with beef mince.

INGREDIENTS

40 g/1½ oz butter

3 tbsp plain flour

300 ml/10 fl oz milk

pinch of ground nutmeg

5 tbsp artichoke pesto or basil pesto

350 g/12 oz spinach, rinsed and drained, coarse stalks removed

1 egg, lightly beaten

450 g/1 lb ricotta cheese

250 g/9 oz cooked ham, diced

2 tomatoes, peeled, deseeded and diced

250 g/9 oz dried no-precook lasagne sheets

4 tbsp freshly grated Parmesan cheese

salt and pepper

1. Melt the butter in a saucepan, stir in the flour and cook over a low heat, stirring constantly, for 1 minute. Remove from the heat and gradually whisk in the milk. Return to the heat and bring to the boil, whisking constantly until thickened and smooth. Remove from the heat and stir in the nutmeg and pesto.

2. Meanwhile, cook the spinach in just the water clinging to the leaves for 5–10 minutes until wilted. Drain, squeeze out the excess moisture and pat dry, then finely chop.

3. Preheat the oven to 200°C/400°F/Gas Mark 6. Stir the egg into the ricotta cheese and season to taste with salt and pepper. Stir in the spinach, ham and tomatoes.

4. Make alternating layers of lasagne, the cheese mixture and the pesto sauce in an ovenproof dish, ending with a layer of lasagne topped with pesto sauce. Cover the dish with foil and bake in the preheated oven for 50 minutes.

5. Remove the dish from the oven, discard the foil and sprinkle the top of the lasagne with the Parmesan cheese. Return to the oven and bake for a further 5 minutes until golden and bubbling. Leave to stand for 5 minutes before serving.

Chicken Ravioli in Tarragon Broth

 SERVES 6

 PREP TIME: 30–45 minutes plus chilling

 COOKING TIME: 1 hour

nutritional information per serving	267 kcals, 8g fat, 4g sat fat, 0.6g total sugars, 1.4g salt

Ravioli are small squares of pasta stuffed with cheese, vegetables or meat. They are a classic Italian dish and usually served with a sauce or delicate broth.

INGREDIENTS

2 litres/3½ pints chicken stock

2 tbsp finely chopped fresh tarragon leaves

freshly grated Parmesan cheese, to serve

pasta dough
125 g/4½ oz flour, plus extra for dusting

2 tbsp fresh tarragon leaves, stems removed

1 egg

1 egg, separated

1 tsp extra virgin olive oil

2–3 tbsp water

pinch of salt

filling
200 g/7 oz cooked chicken, coarsely chopped

½ tsp grated lemon rind

2 tbsp chopped mixed fresh tarragon, chives and parsley

4 tbsp whipping cream

salt and pepper

1. To make the pasta, combine the flour, tarragon and salt in a food processor or blender. Beat together the egg, egg yolk, oil and 2 tablespoons of water. With the machine running, pour in the egg mixture and process until it forms a ball. Wrap and chill for 30 minutes. Reserve the egg white.

2. To make the filling, put the chicken, lemon rind and mixed herbs in a food processor or blender and season to taste with salt and pepper. Chop finely. Do not overprocess. Scrape into a bowl and stir in the cream.

3. Divide the pasta dough in half. Cover one half and roll out the other half on a floured surface to less than 1.5 mm/¹⁄₁₆ inch. Cut out rectangles measuring about 10 x 5 cm/4 x 2 inches. Place a teaspoon of filling on one half of each rectangle. Brush the edges with egg white and fold in half. Press the edges to seal. Arrange on a baking sheet dusted with flour. Repeat with the remaining dough. Allow the ravioli to dry for about 15 minutes or chill for 1–2 hours in the refrigerator.

4. Bring a large saucepan of water to the boil. Drop in half of the ravioli and cook for 12–15 minutes, or until just tender. Drain on a tea towel while cooking the remainder.

5. Meanwhile, put the stock and tarragon in a large saucepan. Bring to the boil, then cover and simmer for 15 minutes. Add the ravioli and simmer for a further 5 minutes. Ladle into warmed bowls and serve immediately with Parmesan cheese.

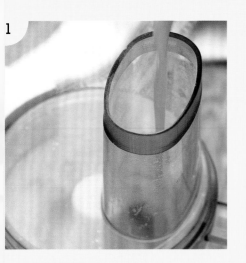

Chicken & Mushroom Lasagne

 SERVES 4–6    PREP TIME: 15 minutes    COOKING TIME: 1½ hours

nutritional information per serving	534 kcals, 25g fat, 11g sat fat, 9g total sugars, 1.1g salt

Lighter than a traditional lasagne, this would be a good dish to serve when you have guests.

INGREDIENTS

2 tbsp olive oil

1 large onion, finely chopped

500 g/1 lb 2 oz fresh chicken or turkey mince

100 g/3½ oz smoked pancetta, chopped

250 g/9 oz chestnut mushrooms, chopped

100 g/3½ oz dried porcini mushrooms, soaked

150 ml/5 fl oz dry white wine

400 g/14 oz canned chopped tomatoes

3 tbsp chopped fresh basil leaves

9 dried no-precook lasagne sheets

3 tbsp finely grated Parmesan cheese

salt and pepper

white sauce
600 ml/1 pint milk

55 g/2 oz butter

55 g/2 oz plain flour

1 bay leaf

1. Preheat the oven to 190°C/375°F/Gas Mark 5. For the white sauce, heat the milk, butter, flour and bay leaf in a saucepan, whisking constantly, until smooth and thick. Season to taste with salt and pepper, cover and leave to stand.

2. Heat the oil in a large saucepan and fry the onion, stirring, for 3–4 minutes. Add the chicken and pancetta and cook for 6–8 minutes. Stir in both types of mushrooms and cook for a further 2–3 minutes.

3. Add the wine and bring to the boil. Pour in the tomatoes and their can juices, cover and simmer for 20 minutes. Stir in the basil.

4. Arrange three of the lasagne sheets in a rectangular ovenproof dish, then spoon over a third of the meat sauce. Remove and discard the bay leaf from the white sauce. Spread a third of the sauce over the meat. Repeat the layers twice more, finishing with a layer of white sauce.

5. Sprinkle with the cheese and bake in the preheated oven for 35–40 minutes, until the topping is golden and bubbling. Serve immediately.

1

2

4

Turkey & Mushroom Cannelloni

 SERVES 4    PREP TIME: **15 minutes**   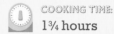 COOKING TIME: **1¾ hours**

nutritional information **per serving**	925 kcals, 48g fat, 26g sat fat, 15g total sugars, 2.6g salt

Cannelloni tubes filled with a delicious mix of mushrooms, chicken, and prosciutto make a wonderful dinner party main course.

INGREDIENTS

butter, for greasing

2 tbsp olive oil

2 garlic cloves, crushed

1 large onion, finely chopped

225 g/8 oz wild mushrooms, sliced

350 g/12 oz fresh turkey mince

115 g/4 oz prosciutto, diced

150 ml/5 fl oz Marsala

200 g/7 oz canned chopped tomatoes

1 tbsp shredded fresh basil leaves

2 tbsp tomato purée

10–12 dried cannelloni tubes

600 ml/1 pint Béchamel Sauce (see page 274)

85 g/3 oz freshly grated Parmesan cheese

salt and pepper

1. Preheat the oven to 190°C/375°F/Gas Mark 5. Lightly grease a large ovenproof dish. Heat the oil in a heavy-based frying pan. Add the garlic, onion and mushrooms and cook over a low heat, stirring frequently, for 8–10 minutes. Add the turkey mince and prosciutto and cook, stirring frequently, for 12 minutes, or until browned all over. Stir in the Marsala, tomatoes and their can juices, basil and tomato purée and cook for 4 minutes. Season to taste with salt and pepper, then cover and simmer for 30 minutes. Uncover, stir and simmer for 15 minutes.

2. Meanwhile, bring a large saucepan of lightly salted water to the boil. Add the cannelloni tubes, bring back to the boil and cook for 8–10 minutes, until tender but still firm to the bite. Using a slotted spoon, transfer the cannelloni tubes to a plate and pat dry with kitchen paper.

3. Using a teaspoon, fill the cannelloni tubes with the turkey and mushroom mixture. Transfer them to the dish. Pour the Béchamel Sauce over them to cover completely and sprinkle with the grated Parmesan cheese.

4. Bake in the preheated oven for 30 minutes, or until golden and bubbling. Serve immediately.

Turkey Pasta Bake

 SERVES 4–6    PREP TIME: 15 minutes    COOKING TIME: 50 minutes

nutritional information per serving	614 kcals, 27g fat, 15g saturated fat, 8g sugar, 1.1g salt

This fail-safe bake is filling, incredibly easy to make and economical – perfect for a midweek family supper.

INGREDIENTS

100 g/3½ oz butter
1 tbsp olive oil
1 onion, finely chopped
450 g/1 lb fresh turkey mince
2 tbsp plain flour
700 ml/1¼ pints milk
1 tsp Dijon mustard
85 g/3 oz Cheddar cheese, grated
280 g/10 oz dried macaroni
2 tbsp chopped fresh parsley
85 g/3 oz fresh breadcrumbs

1. Melt 25 g/1 oz of the butter with the oil in a frying pan. Add the onion and cook over a low heat, stirring occasionally, for 5 minutes until soft. Add the turkey, increase the heat to medium and cook, stirring frequently, for 7–8 minutes, until evenly browned. Remove the pan from the heat, transfer the turkey and onion to a bowl with a slotted spoon and set aside.

2. Melt 40 g/1½ oz of the remaining butter in a saucepan, stir in the flour and cook, stirring constantly, for 1 minute. Remove the pan from the heat and gradually whisk in the milk, then return to the heat and bring to the boil, whisking constantly until thickened. Remove the pan from the heat and stir in the mustard, turkey mixture and 55 g/2 oz of the cheese.

3. Preheat the oven to 180°C/350°F/Gas Mark 4. Bring a large saucepan of lightly salted water to the boil. Add the pasta, bring back to the boil and cook for 8–10 minutes, until tender but still firm to the bite. Drain and stir into the turkey mixture with the parsley.

4. Spoon the mixture into an ovenproof dish, sprinkle with the breadcrumbs and remaining cheese and dot with the remaining butter. Bake in the preheated oven for 25 minutes until golden and bubbling. Serve immediately.

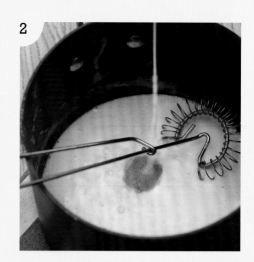

Turkey Manicotti

SERVES 4   PREP TIME: 20 minutes   COOKING TIME: 30–40 minutes

nutritional information per serving	606 kcals, 30g fat, 14g sat fat, 7g total sugars, 1.1g salt

Manicotti are large pasta shells that make a change from smaller cannelloni in this quick-to-prepare dish.

INGREDIENTS

1 tbsp olive oil

450 g/1 lb fresh turkey mince

225 g/8 oz ricotta cheese

55 g/2 oz mozzarella cheese, grated

60 g/2¼ oz freshly grated Parmesan cheese

2 eggs, lightly beaten

2 tbsp chopped fresh flat-leaf parsley

6 dried manicotti

1 quantity Basic Tomato Sauce (see page 272)

salt and pepper

1. Preheat the oven to 180°C/350°F/Gas Mark 4. Heat the oil in a frying pan, add the turkey and cook over a medium heat, stirring frequently, for 6–8 minutes, until evenly browned. Remove the pan from the heat and carefully drain off any fat.

2. Mix the ricotta cheese, mozzarella cheese, 40 g/1½ oz of the Parmesan cheese, the eggs and parsley together in a bowl, season to taste with salt and pepper and stir in the turkey.

3. Bring a large saucepan of lightly salted water to the boil. Add the pasta in two batches, bring back to the boil and cook for 2 minutes. Remove with a slotted spoon. Divide the turkey mixture between the manicotti and put them into an ovenproof dish in a single layer, packing them closely together.

4. Spoon the tomato sauce evenly over the manicotti, sprinkle with the remaining Parmesan cheese and bake for 20–30 minutes, until golden and bubbling. Serve immediately.

SOMETHING
DIFFERENT
This versatile
dish can also
be made with
chicken or beef
mince, or with
chopped spinach
for a vegetarian
version.

Pasticcio

 SERVES 4

 PREP TIME:
15 minutes

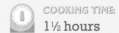 COOKING TIME:
1½ hours

nutritional information
per serving | 523 kcals, 26g fat, 11g saturated fat, 8g sugar, 0.9g salt

This recipe shares its origins with a traditional Greek bake made with lamb. It is delicious served hot or cold.

INGREDIENTS

1 tbsp olive oil
1 onion, chopped
2 garlic cloves, finely chopped
450 g/1 lb fresh lamb mince
2 tbsp tomato purée
2 tbsp plain flour
300 ml/10 fl oz chicken stock
1 tsp ground cinnamon
115 g/4 oz dried macaroni
2 beef tomatoes, sliced
300 ml/10 fl oz Greek yogurt
2 eggs, lightly beaten
salt and pepper

1. Preheat the oven to 190°C/375°F/Gas Mark 5. Heat the oil in a large heavy-based frying pan. Add the onion and garlic and cook over a low heat, stirring occasionally, for 5 minutes, or until softened. Add the lamb and cook, breaking it up with a wooden spoon, until browned all over. Add the tomato purée and sprinkle in the flour. Cook, stirring, for 1 minute, then stir in the stock. Season to taste with salt and pepper and stir in the cinnamon. Bring to the boil, reduce the heat, cover and cook for 25 minutes.

2. Meanwhile, bring a large saucepan of lightly salted water to the boil. Add the pasta, bring back to the boil and cook for 8–10 minutes, until tender but still firm to the bite.

3. Drain the pasta and stir into the lamb mixture. Spoon into a large ovenproof dish and arrange the tomato slices on top. Beat together the yogurt and eggs then spoon over the lamb evenly. Bake in the preheated oven for 1 hour until golden and bubbling. Serve immediately.

VARIATION

Pasticcio doesn't have to be made with lamb. It is also delicious made with minced turkey or chicken.

Mixed Meat Lasagne

 SERVES 6　　 PREP TIME: 15 minutes　　 COOKING TIME: 1¾ hours

nutritional information per serving	929 kcals, 57g fat, 30g saturated fat, 10.5g sugar, 1.9g salt

It is not at all unusual in Italy to use a mixture of minced beef and pork when making a baked lasagne.

INGREDIENTS

1 onion, chopped

1 carrot, chopped

1 celery stick, chopped

85 g/3 oz pancetta, chopped

175 g/6 oz fresh beef mince

175 g/6 oz fresh pork mince

3 tbsp olive oil

100 ml/3½ fl oz red wine

150 ml/5 fl oz beef stock

1 tbsp tomato purée

1 bay leaf

1 clove

150 ml/5 fl oz milk

400 g/14 oz dried no pre-cook lasagne sheets

600 ml/1 pint Béchamel Sauce (see page 274)

140 g/5 oz freshly grated Parmesan cheese

140 g/5 oz mozzarella cheese, diced

55 g/2 oz butter, diced

salt and pepper

1. Mix together the onion, carrot, celery, pancetta, beef and pork in a large bowl. Heat the oil in a large heavy-based frying pan, add the meat mixture and cook over a medium heat, breaking up the meat with a wooden spoon, until it is browned all over. Pour in the wine, then bring to the boil and cook until reduced. Pour in 125 ml/4 fl oz of the stock, bring to the boil and cook until reduced.

2. Mix together the tomato purée and remaining stock in a small bowl, then add to the frying pan with the bay leaf and clove. Season to taste with salt and pepper and pour in the milk. Cover and simmer for 1 hour.

3. Preheat the oven to 200°C/400°F/Gas Mark 6. Remove and discard the bay leaf and the clove from the meat sauce. In a large ovenproof dish, make alternate layers of lasagne sheets, meat sauce, Béchamel Sauce, half the Parmesan cheese and the mozzarella cheese. Finish with a layer of Béchamel Sauce and sprinkle with the remaining Parmesan cheese.

4. Dot the top of the lasagne with butter and bake in the preheated oven for 25 minutes, or until golden and bubbling. Serve immediately.

Spinach & Tomato Tortellini Soup

 SERVES 4

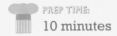 PREP TIME:
10 minutes

 COOKING TIME:
25 minutes

nutritional information per serving	512 kcals, 22g fat, 6g sat fat, 11g total sugars, 1.7g salt

Serve this tasty soup with crusty bread for a filling meal-in-a-bowl lunch for the family.

INGREDIENTS

4 tbsp olive oil

1 onion, thinly sliced

2 garlic cloves, finely chopped

850 ml/1½ pints chicken stock

500 g/1 lb 2 oz fresh or frozen chicken or pork tortellini

400 g/14 oz canned chopped tomatoes

1 tbsp sun-dried tomato purée

400 g/14 oz canned borlotti beans, drained and rinsed

350 g/12 oz spinach, coarse stalks removed, rinsed and drained

2 tbsp chopped fresh flat-leaf parsley

salt and pepper

freshly grated Parmesan cheese, to serve

1. Heat the oil in a saucepan, add the onion and garlic and cook over a low heat, stirring occasionally, for 5 minutes until soft. Pour in the stock, increase the heat to medium and bring to the boil.

2. Add the tortellini and cook for 5 minutes, then reduce the heat, add the tomatoes and their can juices, tomato purée and beans and season to taste with salt and pepper. Reduce the heat and simmer for a further 5 minutes. Stir in the spinach and parsley and cook for 1–2 minutes until the spinach is just wilted. Remove from the heat and serve immediately, with the cheese separately.

SOMETHING
DIFFERENT
For a vegetarian
version, substitute
tortellini stuffed
with ricotta cheese
or pumpkin
purée and use
vegetable rather
than chicken
stock.

Parmesan-filled Tortellini Salad

 SERVES 4

 PREP TIME: 15 minutes

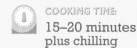 COOKING TIME: 15–20 minutes plus chilling

nutritional information per serving	591 kcals, 42g fat, 8g sat fat, 13g total sugars, 2.6g salt

This salad works just as well as a side dish as it does as a main course and it's also perfect for picnics.

INGREDIENTS

100 ml/3½ fl oz olive oil

1 onion, thinly sliced

1 red pepper, deseeded and thinly sliced

3 tbsp balsamic vinegar

1 tbsp chopped fresh thyme

450 g/1 lb tricolour Parmesan cheese tortellini

350 g/12 oz canned or bottled artichoke hearts, drained and sliced

8 cherry tomatoes, halved

115 g/4 oz black olives, stoned and coarsely chopped

salt and pepper

1. Heat 2 tablespoons of the oil in a frying pan, add the onion and red pepper and cook over a low heat, stirring occasionally, for 8–10 minutes until the onion is just beginning to colour. Stir in the vinegar and thyme, season to taste with salt and remove the pan from the heat.

2. Bring a large saucepan of lightly salted water to the boil. Add the pasta, bring back to the boil and cook for 8–10 minutes until tender but still firm to the bite. Drain well, tip the pasta into a large bowl, add 2 tablespoons of the remaining oil and toss.

3. Add the artichoke hearts, tomatoes and olives to the bowl. Add the pasta and the remaining oil, season to taste with salt and pepper and toss. Add the reserved onion and red pepper mixture and toss again. Cover with clingfilm and chill in the refrigerator for at least 2 hours before serving.

GOES WELL WITH
This quantity
would serve
6-8 as a side
dish and would
be delicious with
grilled chicken,
steak or poached
fish.

Spinach & Ricotta Cannelloni

 SERVES 4    PREP TIME: 20 minutes    COOKING TIME: 40–45 minutes

nutritional information **per serving**	591 kcals, 28g fat, 16g saturated fat, 9g sugar, 1.1g salt

Cannelloni started life as sheets of pasta (lasagne), which were rolled around a filling, but now tubes of pasta, ready for stuffing are available.

INGREDIENTS

melted butter, for greasing

12 dried cannelloni tubes, each about 7.5 cm/3 inches long

salt and pepper

filling

140 g/5 oz frozen spinach, thawed and drained

115 g/4 oz ricotta cheese

1 egg

3 tbsp grated pecorino cheese

pinch of freshly grated nutmeg

cheese sauce

25 g/1 oz butter

2 tbsp plain flour

600 ml/1 pint hot milk

85 g/3 oz Gruyère cheese, grated

1. Preheat the oven to 180°C/350°F/Gas Mark 4. Grease a rectangular ovenproof dish with the melted butter.

2. Bring a large saucepan of lightly salted water to the boil. Add the pasta, bring back to the boil and cook for 6–7 minutes, until nearly tender. Drain and rinse, then spread out on a clean tea towel.

3. For the filling, put the spinach and ricotta into a food processor or blender and process briefly until combined. Add the egg and pecorino cheese and process to a smooth paste. Transfer to a bowl, add the nutmeg and season to taste with salt and pepper.

4. Spoon the filling into a piping bag fitted with a 1-cm/½-inch nozzle. Carefully open a cannelloni tube and pipe in a little of the filling. Place the filled tube in the prepared dish and repeat.

5. For the cheese sauce, melt the butter in a saucepan. Add the flour to the butter and cook over a low heat, stirring constantly, for 1 minute. Remove from the heat and gradually stir in the hot milk. Return to the heat and bring to the boil, stirring constantly. Simmer over a low heat, stirring frequently, for 10 minutes, until thickened and smooth.

6. Remove from the heat, stir in the Gruyère cheese and season to taste with salt and pepper.

7. Spoon the cheese sauce over the filled cannelloni. Cover the dish with foil and bake in the preheated oven for 20–25 minutes. Serve immediately.

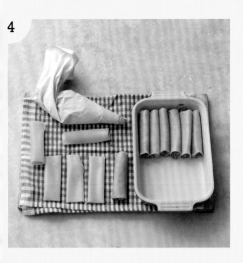

Pumpkin Ravioli

 SERVES 4

 PREP TIME:
30 minutes
plus chilling

 COOKING TIME:
30-35 minutes

nutritional information per serving	452 kcals, 16g fat, 5g saturated fat, 3g sugar, 0.9g salt

This fabulous filled pasta is a favourite in Emilia-Romagna, a region of northern Italy that is famous for its pasta.

INGREDIENTS

300 g/10½ oz durum wheat flour, plus extra for dusting
2 eggs
1 tbsp oil
½ tsp salt
1 tsp vinegar
3–4 tbsp water

filling
1 tbsp olive oil
450 g/1 lb pumpkin, cubed
1 shallot, finely diced
125 ml/4 fl oz water, plus extra for brushing
55 g/2 oz grated Parmesan cheese
1 egg
1 tbsp finely chopped fresh parsley
salt and pepper

1. Knead the flour, eggs, oil, salt, vinegar and water into a silky-smooth dough. Wrap the dough in clingfilm and chill in the refrigerator for 1 hour.

2. For the filling, heat the olive oil in a saucepan, add the pumpkin and shallot and sauté for 2-3 minutes, or until the shallot is translucent. Add the water and cook the pumpkin for 15-20 minutes, or until the liquid evaporates. Cool slightly, then mix with the cheese, egg and parsley. Season to taste with salt and pepper.

3. Divide the dough in half. Thinly roll out both pieces. Place small spoonfuls of the pumpkin mixture about 4 cm/1½ inches apart on one sheet of dough. Brush a little water on the spaces in between. Lay the second sheet of dough on top and press down around each piece of filling.

4. Use a pastry wheel to cut out squares and press the edges together with a fork. Leave the ravioli to dry for 30 minutes, then bring a large saucepan of lightly salted water to the boil. Add the ravioli, bring back to the boil and cook over a medium heat for 8-10 minutes, until tender, but still firm to the bite. Remove the ravioli with a slotted spoon and drain well on kitchen paper. Serve immediately.

Mushroom Cannelloni

 SERVES 4    PREP TIME: 15 minutes   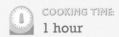 COOKING TIME: 1 hour

nutritional information **per serving** | 866 kcals, 51g fat, 16g sat fat, 13g total sugars, 1.5g salt

This dish is perfect for real mushroom-lovers. You can use any combination of wild mushrooms, you wish. Porcini especially add an extra strong and nutty flavour.

INGREDIENTS

12 dried cannelloni tubes

6 tbsp olive oil, plus extra for brushing

1 onion, finely chopped

2 garlic cloves, finely chopped

800 g/1 lb 12 oz canned chopped tomatoes

1 tbsp tomato purée

8 black olives, stoned and chopped

25 g/1 oz butter

450 g/1 lb wild mushrooms, finely chopped

85 g/3 oz fresh breadcrumbs

150 ml/5 fl oz milk

225 g/8 oz ricotta cheese

6 tbsp freshly grated Parmesan cheese

2 tbsp pine kernels

2 tbsp flaked almonds

salt and pepper

1. Preheat the oven to 190°C/375°F/Gas Mark 5. Bring a large saucepan of lightly salted water to the boil. Add the cannelloni tubes, return to the boil and cook for 8–10 minutes, or until tender but still firm to the bite. With a slotted spoon, transfer the cannelloni tubes to a plate and pat dry. Brush a large ovenproof dish with oil.

2. Heat 2 tablespoons of the oil in a frying pan, add the onion and half the garlic and cook over a low heat for 5 minutes, or until softened. Add the tomatoes and their can juices, tomato purée and olives and season to taste with salt and pepper. Bring to the boil and cook for 3–4 minutes. Pour the sauce into the ovenproof dish.

3. To make the filling, melt the butter in a heavy-based frying pan. Add the mushrooms and remaining garlic and cook over a medium heat, stirring frequently, for 3–5 minutes, or until tender.

4. Remove the frying pan from the heat. Mix the breadcrumbs, milk and remaining oil together in a large bowl, then stir in the ricotta, the mushroom mixture and 4 tablespoons of the Parmesan cheese. Season to taste with salt and pepper.

5. Fill the cannelloni tubes with the mushroom mixture and place them in the prepared dish. Brush with oil and sprinkle with the remaining Parmesan cheese, the pine kernels and almonds. Bake in the preheated oven for 25 minutes until golden and bubbling. Serve immediately.

2

2

3

Broccoli & Mascarpone Cannelloni

 SERVES 4

 PREP TIME:
20 minutes

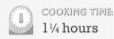 COOKING TIME:
1¼ hours

nutritional information per serving	959 kcals, 59g fat, 25g sat fat, 20g total sugars, 1g salt

This is so rich and delicious that it provides the perfect solution if you're entertaining meat eaters and vegetarians alike – just ensure you check all packaging for animal by-products for your vegetarian guests!

INGREDIENTS

12 dried cannelloni tubes

6 tbsp olive oil, plus extra for brushing

4 shallots, finely chopped

1 garlic clove, finely chopped

600 g/1 lb 5 oz plum tomatoes, peeled, deseeded and chopped

3 red peppers, deseeded and chopped

1 tbsp sun-dried tomato paste

1 tbsp shredded fresh basil leaves

450 g/1 lb broccoli, broken into florets

85 g/3 oz fresh breadcrumbs

150 ml/5 fl oz milk

225 g/8 oz mascarpone cheese

pinch of freshly grated nutmeg

6 tbsp freshly grated pecorino cheese

2 tbsp flaked almonds

salt and pepper

1. Preheat the oven to 190°C/375°F/Gas Mark 5. Bring a large saucepan of lightly salted water to the boil. Add the pasta, bring back to the boil and cook for 8–10 minutes, or until tender but still firm to the bite. Transfer the pasta to a plate and pat dry with kitchen paper. Brush a large ovenproof dish with oil.

2. Heat 2 tablespoons of the oil in a frying pan. Add the shallots and garlic and cook over a low heat for 5 minutes, or until softened. Add the tomatoes, peppers and sun-dried tomato paste and season to taste with salt and pepper. Bring to the boil, then reduce the heat and simmer for 20 minutes. Stir in the basil and pour the sauce into the dish.

3. While the sauce is cooking, place the broccoli in a saucepan of lightly salted boiling water and cook for 10 minutes, or until tender. Drain, then process to a purée in a food processor or blender.

4. Mix together the breadcrumbs, milk and remaining oil in a large bowl, then stir in the mascarpone cheese, nutmeg, broccoli purée and 4 tablespoons of the pecorino cheese. Season to taste with salt and pepper.

5. Fill the cannelloni tubes with the broccoli mixture and place them in the prepared dish. Brush with oil and sprinkle with the remaining pecorino cheese and the almonds. Bake in the preheated oven for 25 minutes until golden and bubbling. Serve immediately.

Spicy Vegetable Lasagne

 SERVES 4    PREP TIME: 15 minutes plus standing time   COOKING TIME: 55 minutes

nutritional information
per serving   534 kcals, 28g fat, 12g saturated fat, 15g sugar, 0.8g salt

This colourful and tasty lasagne has layers of diced and sliced vegetables in tomato sauce, all topped with a rich cheese sauce.

INGREDIENTS

1 aubergine, sliced
3 tbsp olive oil
2 garlic cloves, crushed
1 red onion, halved and sliced
3 mixed peppers, deseeded and diced
225 g/8 oz mushrooms, sliced
2 celery sticks, sliced
1 courgette, diced
½ tsp chilli powder
½ tsp ground cumin
2 tomatoes, chopped
300 ml/10 fl oz passata
3 tbsp chopped fresh basil
8 dried no pre-cook lasagne sheets
salt and pepper

cheese sauce
2 tbsp butter
1 tbsp flour
150 ml/5 fl oz vegetable stock
300 ml/10 fl oz milk
75 g/2¾ oz Cheddar cheese, grated
1 tsp Dijon mustard
1 egg, beaten

1. Place the aubergine slices in a colander, sprinkle with salt and leave for 20 minutes. Rinse under cold water, drain and reserve.

2. Preheat the oven to 180°C/350°F/Gas Mark 4. Heat the oil in a saucepan. Add the garlic and onion and sauté for 1–2 minutes. Add the peppers, mushrooms, celery and courgette and cook, stirring constantly, for 3–4 minutes.

3. Stir in the chilli powder and cumin and cook for 1 minute. Mix in the tomatoes, passata and 2 tablespoons of the basil and season to taste with salt and pepper.

4. For the sauce, melt the butter in a saucepan. Stir in the flour and cook for 1 minute. Remove from the heat, gradually stir in the stock and milk, return to the heat, then add half the cheese and all the mustard. Boil, stirring, until thickened. Stir in the remaining basil. Remove from the heat and stir in the egg.

5. Place half the lasagne sheets in an ovenproof dish. Top with half the vegetable and tomato sauce, then half the aubergines. Repeat and then spoon the cheese sauce on top. Sprinkle with the remaining cheese and bake in the preheated oven for 40 minutes, until golden and bubbling. Serve immediately.

3

4

5

Tuna Pasta Bake

 SERVES 4

 PREP TIME:
20 minutes

 COOKING TIME:
35 minutes

nutritional information per serving	600 kcals, 27g fat, 13g sat fat, 8g total sugars, 2.6g salt

Ever since canned condensed soups were invented in the United States in 1897, they have been used in casserole cooking. The most popular of these meals continues to be Tuna Pasta Bake.

INGREDIENTS

200 g/7 oz dried tagliatelle

25 g/1 oz butter

55 g/2 oz fresh breadcrumbs

400 ml/14 fl oz canned condensed cream of mushroom soup

125 ml/4 fl oz milk

2 celery sticks, chopped

1 red and 1 green pepper, deseeded and chopped

140 g/5 oz mature Cheddar cheese, roughly grated

2 tbsp chopped fresh parsley

200 g/7 oz canned tuna in oil, drained and flaked

salt and pepper

1. Preheat the oven to 200°C/400°F/Gas Mark 6. Bring a large pan of lightly salted water to the boil. Add the pasta and cook for 2 minutes fewer than specified on the packet instructions.

2. Meanwhile, melt the butter in a separate small saucepan over a medium heat. Stir in the breadcrumbs, then remove from the heat and reserve.

3. Drain the pasta thoroughly and reserve. Pour the soup into the pasta pan over a medium heat, then stir in the milk, celery, peppers, half the cheese and all the parsley. Add the tuna and gently stir in so that the flakes don't break up. Season to taste with salt and pepper. Heat just until small bubbles appear around the edge of the mixture – do not boil.

4. Stir the pasta into the pan and use two forks to mix all the ingredients together. Spoon the mixture into an ovenproof dish and spread out. Stir the remaining cheese into the buttered breadcrumbs, then sprinkle over the top of the pasta mixture. Bake in the preheated oven for 20–25 minutes, until golden and bubbling. Leave to stand for 5 minutes before serving.

Salmon Lasagne Rolls

 SERVES 4    PREP TIME: 15 minutes   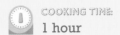 COOKING TIME: 1 hour

nutritional information per serving	487 kcals, 22g fat, 9g saturated fat, 9g sugar, 0.6g salt

This attractive and colourful dish is much easier to make than you might think and is well worth a little extra time.

INGREDIENTS

8 sheets dried lasagne verde

25 g/1 oz butter

1 onion, sliced

½ red pepper, deseeded and chopped

1 courgette, diced

1 tsp chopped fresh ginger

125 g/4½ oz oyster mushrooms, torn into pieces

225 g/8 oz salmon fillet, skinned and cut into chunks

3 tbsp dry sherry

2 tsp cornflour

vegetable oil, for brushing

3 tbsp plain flour

425 ml/15 fl oz milk

25 g/1 oz finely grated Cheddar cheese

1 tbsp fresh white breadcrumbs

salt and pepper

1. Bring a large saucepan of lightly salted water to the boil. Add the pasta, bring back to the boil and cook for 8–10 minutes, until tender but still firm to the bite. Remove with tongs and drain on a clean tea towel.

2. Melt half the butter in a saucepan. Add the onion and cook over a low heat, stirring occasionally, for 5 minutes, until softened. Add the red pepper, courgette and ginger and cook, stirring occasionally, for 10 minutes. Add the mushrooms and salmon and cook for 2 minutes, then mix together the sherry and cornflour and stir into the pan. Cook for a further 4 minutes, until the fish is opaque and flakes easily. Season to taste with salt and pepper and remove the pan from the heat.

3. Preheat the oven to 200°C/400°F/Gas Mark 6. Brush an ovenproof dish with oil.

4. Melt the remaining butter in another pan. Stir in the flour and cook, stirring constantly, for 2 minutes. Gradually stir in the milk, then cook, stirring constantly, for 10 minutes. Remove the pan from the heat, stir in half the Cheddar cheese and season to taste with salt and pepper.

5. Spoon the salmon filling along one of the shorter sides of each sheet of lasagne. Roll up and place in the prepared dish. Pour the sauce over the rolls and sprinkle with the breadcrumbs and remaining cheese. Bake in the preheated oven for 15–20 minutes, until golden and bubbling. Serve immediately.

Layered Salmon & Prawn Spaghetti

 SERVES 6

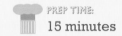 PREP TIME: 15 minutes

 COOKING TIME: 25–30 minutes

nutritional information per serving	573 kcals, 29g fat, 16g saturated fat, 4g sugar, 2.4g salt

The wonderful flavours of succulent prawns and delicate oak-smoked salmon make this simple dish a treat.

INGREDIENTS

350 g/12 oz dried spaghetti

70 g/2½ oz butter, plus extra for greasing

200 g/7 oz smoked salmon, cut into strips

280 g/10 oz large cooked prawns, peeled and deveined

300 ml/10 fl oz Béchamel Sauce (see page 274)

115 g/4 oz freshly grated Parmesan cheese

salt

rocket, to garnish

1. Preheat the oven to 180°C/350°F/Gas Mark 4. Grease a large oven-proof dish with butter and set aside.

2. Bring a large saucepan of lightly salted water to the boil. Add the pasta, bring back to the boil and cook for 8–10 minutes, until tender but still firm to the bite. Drain well, return to the saucepan, add 55 g/2 oz of the butter and toss well.

3. Spoon half the spaghetti into the prepared dish, cover with the strips of smoked salmon, then top with the prawns. Pour over half the béchamel sauce and sprinkle with half the cheese. Add the rest of the spaghetti, cover with the remaining sauce and sprinkle with the remaining cheese. Dice the reserved butter and dot it over the surface.

4. Bake in the preheated oven for 15 minutes, until golden and bubbling. Serve immediately, garnished with rocket.

2

3

3

GOES WELL WITH
An avocado and tomato salad with a yogurt dressing matches the luxurious flavours of this baked pasta dish.

Macaroni & Seafood Bake

 SERVES 4

 PREP TIME:
10 minutes

 COOKING TIME:
50 minutes

nutritional information per serving	825 kcals, 42g fat, 21g saturated fat, 12g sugar, 2.7g salt

Fennel imparts a delicate anise flavour to dishes and goes particularly well with fish.

INGREDIENTS

350 g/12 oz dried macaroni

85 g/3 oz butter, plus extra for greasing

2 small fennel bulbs, trimmed and thinly sliced

175 g/6 oz mushrooms, thinly sliced

175 g/6 oz cooked peeled prawns

pinch of cayenne pepper

600 ml/1 pint Béchamel Sauce (see page 274)

55 g/2 oz freshly grated Parmesan cheese

2 large tomatoes, halved and sliced

olive oil, for brushing

1 tsp dried oregano

salt

1. Preheat the oven to 180°C/350°F/Gas Mark 4. Bring a large saucepan of lightly salted water to the boil. Add the pasta, bring back to the boil and cook for 8–10 minutes, until tender but still firm to the bite.

2. Drain and return to the saucepan. Add 25 g/1 oz of the butter to the pasta, cover, shake the saucepan and keep warm.

3. Melt the remaining butter in a separate saucepan. Add the fennel and cook for 3–4 minutes. Stir in the mushrooms and cook for a further 2 minutes. Stir in the prawns, then remove the pan from the heat. Stir the cooked pasta, cayenne pepper and prawn mixture into the Béchamel Sauce.

4. Grease a large ovenproof dish, then pour the mixture into the dish and spread evenly. Sprinkle over the Parmesan cheese and arrange the tomato slices in a ring around the edge. Brush the tomatoes with oil, then sprinkle over the oregano. Bake in the preheated oven for 25 minutes until golden and bubbling. Serve immediately.

Sauces

Simple Butter Sauce

 SERVES 4    PREP TIME: 15 minutes    COOKING TIME: 15 minutes

nutritional information per serving	562 kcals, 26g fat, 15g saturated fat, 2g sugar, 0.5g salt

Fresh-tasting and made in minutes, this is a great way to serve any long pasta, such as linguine, for a midweek family meal.

INGREDIENTS

400 g/14 oz dried long pasta

115 g/4 oz butter

8 sage leaves, finely chopped

8 basil leaves, finely chopped

½ bunch fresh flat-leaf parsley, finely chopped

6 fresh thyme sprigs, finely chopped

1 small bunch of chives, snipped

salt and pepper

freshly grated Parmesan cheese, to serve

1. Bring a large saucepan of lightly salted water to the boil. Add the pasta, bring back to the boil and cook for 8–10 minutes, until tender but still firm to the bite.

2. Just before the pasta is ready, melt the butter in a frying pan over a low heat. Drain the pasta and pour the melted butter into the pan with the pasta. Add all the herbs, season to taste with salt and pepper and toss until the pasta strands are coated and glistening.

3. Divide between warmed plates and serve immediately, with the Parmesan cheese handed separately.

SOMETHING
DIFFERENT
Vary the herbs to suit
your personal taste,
but be careful with
very pungent ones,
such as tarragon and
marjoram.

Bolognese sauce

 SERVES 4

 PREP TIME:
15 minutes
plus soaking

 COOKING TIME:
1¼ hours

nutritional information per serving	316 kcals, 19g fat, 8.5g sat fat, 6.5g total sugars, 0.7g salt

This Italian classic is another recipe that benefits from longer simmering at a low temperature – perfect if your guests are late!

INGREDIENTS

25 g/1 oz dried porcini
125 ml/4 fl oz lukewarm water
1 tbsp butter
55 g/2 oz pancetta, diced
1 small onion, finely chopped
1 garlic clove, finely chopped
2 small carrots, finely diced
2 celery sticks, finely diced
300 g/10½ oz beef mince
1 pinch sugar
freshly grated nutmeg
1 tbsp tomato purée
125 ml/4 fl oz red wine
250 g/9 oz passata
salt and pepper

1. Soak the porcini in the water for 20 minutes.

2. Melt the butter in a saucepan, add the pancetta and fry for 3-4 minutes, or until just beginning to brown.

3. Add the onion and garlic and fry until the onion is translucent. Stir in the carrots and celery and cook for a few minutes, stirring frequently.

4. Add the beef and fry, stirring constantly. Season to taste with salt and pepper, a pinch of sugar and some nutmeg. Stir in the tomato purée and cook for a minute or two, then add the wine. Mix in the passata. Drain and thinly slice the porcini and add them to the sauce. Pour the soaking water through a fine sieve into the sauce, then thicken by cooking it over a low heat for 1 hour. Use as required.

Basic Tomato Sauce

 SERVES 4   PREP TIME: 15 minutes   COOKING TIME: 25–30 minutes

nutritional information per serving	124 kcals, 11g fat, 4g sat fat, 5g total sugars, 0.2g salt

There is no question that this is Italy's most favourite sauce for serving with pasta as well as other ingredients.

INGREDIENTS

25 g/1 oz butter

2 tbsp olive oil

1 onion, finely chopped

1 garlic clove, finely chopped

1 celery stick, finely chopped

400 g/14 oz canned chopped tomatoes or 500 g/1 lb 2 oz plum tomatoes, peeled, cored and chopped

2 tbsp tomato purée

brown sugar, to taste

1 tbsp chopped fresh herbs and/or 1–2 tsp dried herbs and/or 1–2 bay leaves

100 ml/3½ fl oz water

salt and pepper

1. Melt the butter with the oil in a saucepan. Add the onion, garlic and celery and cook over a low heat, stirring occasionally, for 5 minutes, until softened.

2. Stir in the tomatoes, tomato purée, sugar to taste, the herbs and water and season to taste with salt and pepper.

3. Increase the heat to medium and bring to the boil, then reduce the heat and simmer, stirring occasionally, for 15–20 minutes, until thickened. Remove the bay leaves, if using. Use as required.

GOES WELL WITH
This all-purpose
sauce may be
served with almost
any kind of pasta,
especially ridged
and curly types
and is also
delicious baked
with ravioli.

Béchamel Sauce

 SERVES 4    PREP TIME: 10 minutes    COOKING TIME: 15 minutes

nutritional information per serving	338 kcals, 29g fat, 18g sat fat, 6g total sugars, 0.3g salt

Béchamel sauce (or white sauce) is one of the classic French sauces. The basic béchamel recipe is a great base to expand on and make other interesting and delicious variations.

INGREDIENTS

300 ml/10 fl oz milk

2 bay leaves

3 cloves

1 small onion

55 g/2 oz butter

40 g/1½ oz plain flour

300 ml/10 fl oz single cream

large pinch of freshly grated nutmeg

salt and pepper

1. Pour the milk into a small saucepan and add the bay leaves. Press the cloves into the onion, add to the saucepan and bring the milk to the boil. Remove the saucepan from the heat and set aside to cool.

2. Strain the milk into a jug and rinse the saucepan. Melt the butter in the saucepan, stir in the flour and cook for 1 minute, stirring. Remove from the heat and gradually pour in the milk, stirring constantly. Cook the sauce for 3 minutes, stirring, then pour in the cream and bring it to the boil. Remove from the heat and season with nutmeg and salt and pepper to taste.

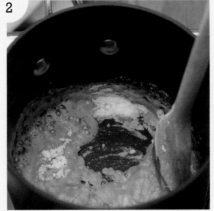

VARIATION
All sorts of ingredients can be added to the basic Béchamel recipe to make interesting sauces which go particularly well with vegetables and fish as well as pasta.

Classic Pesto

 SERVES 4    PREP TIME: 15 minutes   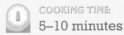 COOKING TIME: 5–10 minutes

nutritional information per serving	144 kcals, 13.5g fat, 3.5g sat fat, 0.3g total sugars, 0.2g salt

Pesto is delicious stirred into pasta, soups and salad dressings. It is available in most supermarkets, but making your own gives a concentrated flavour.

INGREDIENTS

40 fresh basil leaves
3 garlic cloves, crushed
25 g/1 oz pine kernels
50 g/1¾ oz Parmesan cheese, finely grated
2–3 tbsp extra virgin olive oil
salt and pepper

1. Rinse the basil leaves and pat them dry with kitchen paper. Put the basil leaves, garlic, pine kernels and cheese into a food processor or blender and blend for 30 seconds or until smooth. Alternatively, pound all of the ingredients in a mortar with a pestle.

2. If you are using a food processor, keep the motor running and slowly add the olive oil. Alternatively, add the oil drop by drop while stirring briskly. Season with salt and pepper to taste. Use as required.

COOK'S NOTE
You can make
this pesto a
day ahead and
keep it in the
refrigerator until
you are ready to
cook the pasta.

Parsley & Almond Pesto

 SERVES 4

 PREP TIME:
15 minutes

 COOKING TIME:
no cooking

nutritional information
per serving | 282 kcals, 28g fat, 5g saturated fat, 0.6g sugar, 0.2g salt

As well as being a slightly sweet and refreshing sauce to serve with pasta, this quick sauce is great with poached fish.

INGREDIENTS

55 g/2 oz flat-leaf parsley,
coarse stalks removed

2 garlic cloves, coarsely chopped

25 g/1 oz blanched almonds

125 ml/4 fl oz olive oil

40 g/1½ oz pecorino cheese,
grated

salt and pepper

1. Put the parsley, garlic and almonds in a food processor or blender, season to taste with salt and pepper and process until very finely chopped.

2. With the motor running on slow speed, gradually add the oil in a slow, steady stream, until a smooth paste forms. Add the cheese and pulse a few times to combine.

3. Taste and adjust the seasoning, if necessary, and heat gently – do not allow to boil. Use as required.

COOK'S NOTE
To make by hand, grind the step 1 ingredients in a mortar with a pestle, then transfer to a bowl. Gradually whisk in the oil with a fork, then stir in the cheese.

Spicy Alfredo Sauce

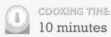
nutritional information **per serving** : 799 kcals, 44g fat, 27g saturated fat, 3g sugar, 0.5g salt

Alfredo di Lelio invented his classic cream, butter and Parmesan sauce in Rome in 1914 and since then it has been modified in dozens of ways.

INGREDIENTS

450 g/1 lb dried fettuccine or other pasta
55 g/2 oz butter
1–2 chillies, finely chopped
200 ml/7 fl oz double cream
55 g/2 oz freshly grated Parmesan cheese
salt and pepper

1. Bring a large saucepan of lightly salted water to the boil. Add the pasta, bring back to the boil and cook for 8–10 minutes, until tender but still firm to the bite.

2. Meanwhile, melt half the butter in another large saucepan, add the chillies and cook over a low heat, stirring occasionally, for 3 minutes. Pour in 150 ml/5 fl oz of the cream, increase the heat to medium and bring to the boil. Reduce the heat and simmer for 1–2 minutes until slightly thickened. Remove the pan from the heat.

3. Drain the pasta and tip it into the pan with the cream sauce. Return to the heat and lightly toss, then add the cheese and the remaining butter and cream. Season to taste with salt and pepper and toss for 2–3 minutes until the pasta is thoroughly coated in the sauce. Remove from the heat and serve immediately.

SOMETHING
DIFFERENT
For a more
substantial dish,
add some strips
of prosciutto or
shredded cooked
chicken in
step 3.

Arrabiata Sauce

 SERVES 4    PREP TIME: 15 minutes   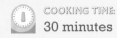 COOKING TIME: 30 minutes

nutritional information per serving	518 kcals, 16g fat, 2.5g sat fat, 6g total sugars, trace salt

Serve this tangy hot tomato sauce with pasta shapes, such as penne, or spaghetti. Unlike many other tomato sauce and pasta dishes, it is not traditionally served with grated Parmesan cheese.

INGREDIENTS

150 ml/5 fl oz dry white wine

1 tbsp sun-dried tomato purée

2 fresh red chillies, deseeded and chopped

2 garlic cloves, finely chopped

4 tbsp chopped fresh flat-leaf parsley

salt and pepper

85 g/3 oz pecorino cheese shavings, to garnish

sugocasa

5 tbsp extra virgin olive oil

450 g/1 lb plum tomatoes, chopped

salt and pepper

1. To make the sugocasa. Heat the oil in a frying pan over a high heat until almost smoking. Add the tomatoes and cook, stirring frequently, for 2–3 minutes.

2. Reduce the heat to low and cook gently for 20 minutes, or until very soft. Season to taste with salt and pepper. Press through a non-metallic sieve with a wooden spoon into a saucepan.

3. Add the wine, tomato purée, chillies and garlic to the sugocasa and bring to the boil. Reduce the heat and simmer gently. Check and adjust the seasoning, then stir in the parsley and the cheese. Use as required.

Chipotle Sauce

SERVES 4

PREP TIME:
45 minutes

COOKING TIME:
15 minutes

nutritional information per serving	166 kcals, 16g fat, 1g sat fat, 3g total sugars, trace salt

Smoking jalapeño chillies to make chipotles gives them a delicious depth of flavour but they do remain quite fiery.

INGREDIENTS

2 ancho chillies, deseeded

1 red pepper

1–2 canned jalapeño or chipotle chillies, drained

5 tablespoons pine kernels

juice of ½ lime

2 garlic cloves, roughly chopped

1 tbsp olive oil

salt

1. Preheat the grill. Meanwhile put the ancho chillies into a bowl, pour in hot water to cover and leave to soak for 30 minutes.

2. Put the red pepper on a baking sheet and place under the grill, turning occasionally, for about 15 minutes, until charred and blistered. Remove with tongs, put into a polythene bag, tie the top and leave to cool.

3. Drain the ancho chillies, reserving 1 tablespoon of the soaking liquid. Peel, deseed and roughly chop the red pepper.

4. Put the ancho chillies, reserved soaking liquid, red pepper, jalapeño chillies, pine kernels, 1 tablespoon of the lime juice and the garlic into a food processor or blender and process to a smooth paste. With the motor running at low speed, add the oil and process until thoroughly combined. If the sauce is too thick, add a little more lime juice and process briefly again. Season to taste with salt and use as required.

1

2

4

FREEZING TIP
Freeze the sauce
in an airtight
container for
1-2 weeks.

Mole Sauce

 SERVES 6–10    PREP TIME: 10 minutes plus soaking    COOKING TIME: 30 minutes

nutritional information per serving	263 kcals, 20g fat, 3.5g saturated fat, 9g sugar, 0.1g salt

Mole is renowned for its surprising pairing of chocolate and chilli. The result is sumptuous rather than strange, with a deep, rich, mellow quality.

INGREDIENTS

9 mixed chillies, soaked in hot water for 30 minutes and drained

1 onion, sliced

2–3 garlic cloves, crushed

85 g/3 oz sesame seeds

85 g/3 oz toasted flaked almonds

1 tsp ground coriander

4 cloves

½ tsp pepper

2–3 tbsp sunflower oil

300 ml/10 fl oz chicken or vegetable stock

450 g/1 lb ripe tomatoes, peeled and chopped

2 tsp ground cinnamon

55 g/2 oz raisins

140 g/5 oz pumpkin seeds

55 g/2 oz plain chocolate, broken into pieces

1 tbsp red wine vinegar

1. Put the chillies into a food processor or blender with the onion, garlic, sesame seeds, almonds, coriander, cloves and pepper and process to form a thick paste.

2. Heat the oil in a saucepan, add the paste, and fry for 5 minutes. Add the stock with the tomatoes, cinnamon, raisins and pumpkin seeds. Bring to the boil, reduce the heat and simmer, stirring occasionally, for 15 minutes.

3. Add the chocolate and vinegar to the sauce. Cook gently for 5 minutes, then use as required.

Creole Sauce

 SERVES 4    PREP TIME: 15 minutes    COOKING TIME: 35–40 minutes

nutritional information per serving	127 kcals, 6.5g fat, 1g saturated fat, 10g sugar, 0.2g salt

Enjoy a taste of the Deep South with this vibrant, spicy sauce, the chopped okra lending it both characteristic flavour and thickness.

INGREDIENTS

2 tbsp sunflower oil

1 red pepper, deseeded and thinly sliced

1 green pepper, deseeded and thinly sliced

1 onion, thinly sliced

2–3 garlic cloves, crushed

1 fresh red chilli, deseeded and chopped

1 tsp ground coriander

1 tsp ground cumin

450 g/1 lb ripe tomatoes, peeled and chopped

300 ml/10 fl oz vegetable stock

115 g/4 oz okra, trimmed and chopped

1 tbsp chopped fresh coriander

salt and pepper

1. Heat the oil in a heavy-based saucepan, add the red pepper, green pepper, onion, garlic and chilli and sauté, stirring frequently, for 3 minutes. Add the ground coriander and cumin and sauté, stirring frequently, for a further 3 minutes.

2. Stir in the tomatoes and stock and bring to the boil. Reduce the heat and simmer, stirring occasionally, for 15 minutes, or until the sauce has reduced slightly.

3. Add the okra to the pan with salt and pepper to taste and simmer for a further 10–15 minutes, or until the sauce has thickened. Stir in the fresh coriander and use as required.

Four Cheese Sauce

SERVES 4

PREP TIME:
15 minutes

COOKING TIME:
8–10 minutes

nutritional information
per serving

879 kcals, 44g fat, 27g sat fat, 2.5g total sugars, 2.5g salt

Unusually, this sauce is actually made in the serving dish containing the drained pasta and must be one of the quickest ever!

INGREDIENTS

450 g/1 lb dried tagliatelle

55 g/2 oz butter

100 g/3½ oz Gorgonzola, crumbled

100 g/3½ oz fontina cheese, cut into narrow julienne strips

100 g/3½ oz Gruyère cheese, cut into julienne strips

100 g/3½ oz Parmesan cheese, cut into julienne strips

salt

1. Bring a large saucepan of lightly salted water to the boil. Add the pasta, bring back to the boil and cook for 8–10 minutes, until tender but still firm to the bite.

2. Meanwhile, put the butter in a heatproof bowl set over a saucepan of barely simmering water. When it has melted, continue to heat it until very hot, but not boiling.

3. Drain the pasta and tip into a warmed serving bowl. Sprinkle with the four cheeses and pour the hot butter over. Toss lightly and serve immediately.

1

2

3

SOMETHING DIFFERENT
You could substitute strips of halloumi for the Gorgonzola for a subtler flavour.

Mushroom Sauce

 SERVES 4    PREP TIME:
10 minutes   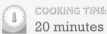 COOKING TIME:
20 minutes

nutritional information per serving	746 kcals, 43g fat, 20g sat fat, 5g total sugars, 0.3g salt

This is a delicious sauce which uses shallots, chestnut mushrooms and double cream and port for a truly luxurious touch.

INGREDIENTS

55 g/2 oz butter

1 tbsp olive oil

6 shallots, sliced

450 g/1 lb chestnut mushrooms, sliced

1 tsp plain flour

150 ml/5 fl oz double cream

2 tbsp port

115 g/4 oz sun-dried tomatoes in oil, drained and chopped

pinch of freshly grated nutmeg

salt and pepper

1. Melt the butter with the oil in a large heavy-based frying pan. Add the shallots and cook over a low heat, stirring occasionally, for 4–5 minutes, or until softened. Add the mushrooms and cook over a low heat for a further 2 minutes. Season to taste with salt and pepper, sprinkle in the flour and cook, stirring, for 1 minute.

2. Remove the frying pan from the heat and gradually stir in the cream and port. Return to the heat, add the sun-dried tomatoes and grated nutmeg and cook over a low heat, stirring occasionally, for 8 minutes. Use as required.

Lemon & Tarragon Sauce

 SERVES 4

 PREP TIME:
5 minutes

 COOKING TIME:
no cooking

nutritional information per serving	200 kcals, 12g fat, 2g sat fat, 0.5g total sugars, trace salt

The sharpness of lemon and the hint of aniseed in tarragon make this a really refreshing combination.

INGREDIENTS

1 small bunch of tarragon
juice of ½ lemon
grated rind of 1 lemon
4 tbsp olive oil
2 garlic cloves, coarsely chopped
4 fresh parsley sprigs
1 bunch of chives
salt

1. Pick off the leaves from the tarragon and put them into a food processor or blender with the lemon juice, lemon rind, oil, garlic, parsley, chives and a generous pinch of salt and process until thoroughly combined. Use as required.

SOMETHING DIFFERENT

For a sweeter flavour, substitute 2 tablespoons of orange juice and the grated rind of ½ an orange for the lemon juice and rind.

Tomato, Mushroom & Bacon Sauce

 SERVES 2　　 PREP TIME: 20 minutes　　 COOKING TIME: 30–35 minutes

nutritional information per serving	231 kcals, 17g fat, 6g sat fat, 9g total sugars, 1.8g salt

In this dish, fresh tomatoes make a delicious Italian-style sauce, which goes particularly well with pasta.

INGREDIENTS

1 tbsp olive oil

1 small onion, finely chopped

1–2 garlic cloves, crushed

350 g/12 oz tomatoes, peeled and chopped

2 tsp tomato purée

2 tbsp water

90 g/3¼ oz lean, rindless bacon, diced

40 g/1½ oz mushrooms, sliced

1 tbsp chopped fresh parsley or 1 tsp chopped fresh coriander

2 tbsp soured cream (optional)

salt and pepper

freshly cooked pasta, to serve

1. Heat the oil in a saucepan over a low heat and fry the onion and garlic gently.

2. Add the tomatoes, tomato purée and water to the mixture in the pan, season with salt and pepper to taste and bring to the boil. Cover and simmer gently for 10 minutes.

3. Heat the bacon gently in a frying pan until the fat runs, add the mushrooms, and continue cooking for 3–4 minutes. Drain off any excess fat.

4. Add the bacon and mushrooms to the tomato mixture, together with the parsley and the soured cream, if using. Reheat the sauce gently then pour over the pasta and toss well. Serve immediately.

Roasted Garlic & Herb Sauce

 SERVES 4

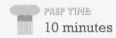 PREP TIME:
10 minutes

 COOKING TIME:
35–40 minutes

nutritional information per serving	72 kcals, 5g fat, 2g saturated fat, 1g sugar, trace salt

Roasting garlic gives it a wonderfully mild flavour and a deliciously creamy texture.

INGREDIENTS

1 garlic bulb

1 tbsp olive oil

2 handfuls of mixed herbs, such as flat-leaf parsley, basil, thyme and sage, coarse stalks removed

3–4 tbsp soured cream

salt and pepper

1. Preheat the oven to 200°C/400°F/Gas Mark 6. Peel the outer papery layers from the garlic bulb but leave the individual cloves intact. Using a sharp knife, cut a 5–10-mm/¼–½-inch slice off the top of the garlic to expose the cloves.

2. Put the bulb into a small ovenproof container, such as a ramekin, and drizzle with the oil. Cover with foil and roast in the preheated oven for 35–40 minutes until the cloves feel soft.

3. Remove from the oven and leave until cool enough to handle, then squeeze out the pulp from each clove into a food processor or blender. Add the herbs and soured cream and process until combined and reheat the sauce gently over a low heat without boiling, if required. Season to taste with salt and pepper and use as required.

COOK'S NOTE
You can buy a
special garlic roaster -
a small terracotta tray
with a bell-shaped
cover. You could also
just wrap the oil-
drizzled garlic bulb
in foil.

Pumpkin Sauce

 SERVES 4    PREP TIME: 15 minutes    COOKING TIME: 1¼ hours

nutritional information per serving	295 kcals, 28g fat, 16g sat fat, 6g total sugars, 0.6g salt

This subtle and unusual sauce has a velvety texture, looks fabulous and tastes simply superb.

INGREDIENTS

55 g/2 oz butter

6 shallots, very finely chopped

800 g/1 lb 12 oz pumpkin, peeled, deseeded and cut into pieces

pinch of freshly grated nutmeg

200 ml/7 fl oz single cream

4 tbsp freshly grated Parmesan cheese

2 tbsp chopped fresh flat-leaf parsley

salt

1. Melt the butter in a large heavy-based saucepan. Add the shallots, sprinkle with a little salt, cover and cook over a very low heat, stirring occasionally, for 30 minutes.

2. Add the pumpkin pieces and season to taste with nutmeg. Cover and cook over a very low heat, stirring occasionally, for 40 minutes, or until the pumpkin is pulpy. Stir in the cream, cheese and parsley and remove the pan from the heat.

3. Stir the pumpkin mixture and add a little boiling water if the mixture seems too thick. Use as required.

VARIATION
Although traditionally made with pumpkin, you could also use butternut or acorn squash for this dish.

Sun-dried Tomato Sauce

 SERVES 4

 PREP TIME:
10 minutes

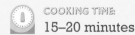 COOKING TIME:
15–20 minutes

nutritional information
per serving

600 kcals, 18g fat, 1.5g sat fat, 13g total sugars, 0.2g salt

Sun-dried tomatoes give this almost instant sauce an intense depth of sweet flavour.

INGREDIENTS

3 tbsp olive oil

2 large onions, sliced

2 celery sticks, thinly sliced

2 garlic cloves, chopped

400 g/14 oz canned chopped tomatoes

125 g/4½ oz sun-dried tomatoes in oil, drained and chopped

2 tbsp tomato purée

1 tbsp dark muscovado sugar

about 150 ml/5 fl oz white wine or water

salt and pepper

1. Heat the oil in a frying pan. Add the onions and celery and cook until translucent. Add the garlic and cook for 1 minute. Stir in all the tomatoes, tomato purée, sugar and wine and season to taste with salt and pepper. Bring to the boil and simmer for 10 minutes. Use as required.

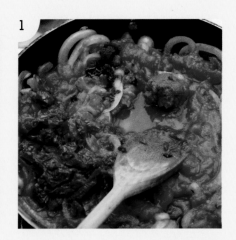

GOES WELL WITH
Use this flavoursome sauce in a meat or vegetable lasagne or serve with any pasta with a robust meaty filling.

Garlic Walnut Sauce

 SERVES 4

 PREP TIME:
15 minutes

 COOKING TIME:
15–20 minutes

nutritional information per serving	311 kcals, 29g fat, 12g sat fat, 3g total sugars, 0.5g salt

This rich pasta sauce is for garlic lovers everywhere. It is quick and easy to prepare and full of flavour.

INGREDIENTS

2 tbsp walnut oil

1 bunch of spring onions, sliced

2 garlic cloves, thinly sliced

225 g/8 oz mushrooms, sliced

225 g/8 oz frozen spinach, thawed and drained

115 g/4 oz full-fat cream cheese with garlic and herbs

4 tbsp single cream

55 g/2 oz unsalted pistachio nuts, chopped

salt and pepper

1. Heat the walnut oil in a large frying pan. Add the spring onions and garlic and fry for 1 minute, or until just softened. Add the mushrooms, stir well, cover and cook over a low heat for 5 minutes, or until just softened but not browned.

2. Add the spinach to the frying pan and cook for 1-2 minutes. Add the cheese and heat until slightly melted. Stir in the cream and pistachio nuts and season to taste with salt and pepper. Cook gently, without letting the mixture come to the boil, until warmed through. Use as required.

GOES WELL WITH

This is especially delicious with pasta filled with cheese and herbs or other greens and is also tasty simply served with ribbon pasta.

Red Wine Sauce

 SERVES 4

 PREP TIME:
15 minutes

 COOKING TIME:
20 minutes

nutritional information per serving	240 kcals, 20g fat, 10g sat fat, 2.5g total sugars, 0.6g salt

Mushrooms are more usually cooked with white wine, but the robust earthy flavour of wild mushrooms is perfectly complemented with red wine in this sauce.

INGREDIENTS

70–100 g/2½–3½ oz butter

350 g/12 oz mixed wild mushrooms, halved or quartered if large

2 garlic cloves, finely chopped

1 tbsp olive oil

4 tbsp tomato purée

250 ml/9 fl oz full-bodied red wine

50 g/1¾ oz black olives, stoned and halved

1 tbsp chopped fresh parsley

salt and pepper

1. Melt 25 g/1 oz of the butter in a large frying pan, add the mushrooms, sprinkle with a little salt and cook over a high heat, stirring occasionally, for 5 minutes.

2. Reduce the heat under the frying pan to low, stir in the garlic and oil and cook for 2 minutes, then stir in the tomato purée and cook for a further 2 minutes.

3. Pour in the wine and cook for about 5 minutes until the alcohol has evaporated. Meanwhile, dice the remaining butter. Add the butter to the pan, 1 piece at a time, gently swirling the pan until the butter has melted. Stir in the olives, season to taste with salt and pepper and remove the pan from the heat. Sprinkle with parsley and use as required.

White Wine Sauce

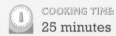
nutritional information per serving	844 kcals, 77g fat, 48g sat fat, 4.5g total sugars, 1.2g salt

This rich, creamy sauce goes well with filled pasta such as ravioli – use a stock that matches the filling for extra flavour.

INGREDIENTS

1 onion, chopped

400 ml/14 fl oz dry white wine

1 litre/1¾ pints vegetable, chicken or fish stock

400 ml/14 fl oz double cream

115 g/4 oz butter

3 tbsp finely chopped flat-leaf parsley

salt and pepper

1. Put the onion in a saucepan, pour in the wine and bring to the boil. Cook over a high heat for 10 minutes until the wine has almost completely evaporated.

2. Pour in the stock, bring to the boil and cook for a further 10 minutes, until it has reduced by two-thirds.

3. Stir in the cream and cook for 5 minutes, then stir in the butter, a little at a time. Add the parsley, season to taste with salt and pepper and use as required.

2

3

3

SOMETHING DIFFERENT

You can vary the herb to match the pasta filling - use tarragon or chervil with chicken, for example, or a mixture of your favourite herbs.

Vodka Sauce

 SERVES 4

 PREP TIME:
5 minutes

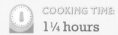 COOKING TIME:
1¼ hours

nutritional information
per serving | 582 kcals, 52g fat, 32g sat fat, 8g total sugars, 0.5g salt

This exotic creamy sauce has become extremely fashionable in the last few years but is surprisingly easy to make.

INGREDIENTS

55 g/2 oz butter
1 onion, finely chopped
125 ml/4 fl oz vodka
800 g/1 lb 12 oz canned chopped tomatoes
300 ml/10 fl oz double cream
salt and pepper

1. Melt the butter in a large saucepan, add the onion, and cook over a low heat, stirring occasionally, for 8–10 minutes until just beginning to colour.

2. Add the vodka and simmer for 10 minutes, then stir in the tomatoes, crushing them gently with a wooden spoon. Simmer, stirring occasionally, for 25 minutes.

3. Stir in the cream, season to taste with salt and pepper and simmer for a further 30 minutes. Do not allow the sauce to boil. Remove from the heat and use as required.

1

2

3

SOMETHING
DIFFERENT
To add a spicy kick,
stir ½ teaspoon of
crushed chillies into
the vodka and leave to
infuse for 10 minutes
before straining the
vodka into the pan.

Spicy Crab Sauce

 SERVES 4   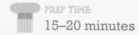 PREP TIME: 15–20 minutes    COOKING TIME: 5-10 minutes

nutritional information
per serving   336 kcals, 22g fat, 3g sat fat, 0.3g total sugars, 0.9g salt

This sauce is probably one of the simplest in the book, yet the result is as impressive as a sauce that takes a long time to prepare.

INGREDIENTS

1 dressed crab, about 450 g/
1 lb (including the shell)
6 tbsp extra-virgin olive oil
1 fresh red chilli, deseeded and
finely chopped
2 garlic cloves, finely chopped
3 tbsp chopped fresh parsley
2 tbsp lemon juice
1 tsp finely grated lemon zest
salt and pepper

1. Scoop the meat from the crab shell into a bowl. Mix the white and brown meat lightly together and set aside.

2. Heat 2 tablespoons of the olive oil in a frying pan. Add the chilli and garlic. Cook for 30 seconds, then add the crab meat, parsley, lemon juice and lemon zest. Stir-fry over a low heat for a further 1 minute, or until the crab meat is just heated through.

3. Add the remaining olive oil to the sauce and season to taste with salt and pepper. Use as required.

Seafood Sauce

 SERVES 4

 PREP TIME:
15 minutes

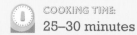 COOKING TIME:
25–30 minutes

nutritional information per serving	232 kcals, 10g fat, 2g sat fat, 0.2g total sugars, 0.9g salt

This is a great pasta sauce for informal entertaining as it is so quick and easy to make.

INGREDIENTS

675 g/1 lb 8 oz fresh clams, or 280 g/10 oz canned clams, drained

2 tbsp olive oil

2 garlic cloves, finely chopped

400 g/14 oz mixed prepared seafood, such as prawns, squid and mussels, defrosted if frozen

150 ml/5 fl oz white wine

150 ml/5 fl oz fish stock

2 tbsp chopped fresh tarragon

salt and pepper

1. If using fresh clams scrub them clean and discard any that are already open.

2. Heat the oil in a large frying pan. Add the garlic and clams and cook for 2 minutes, shaking the pan to ensure that all of the clams are coated in the oil. Add the remaining seafood to the pan and cook for a further 2 minutes.

3. Pour the wine and stock over the mixed seafood and garlic and bring to the boil. Cover the pan, then lower the heat and simmer for 8–10 minutes, or until the shells open. Discard any clams or mussels that do not open.

4. Stir the tarragon into the sauce and season to taste with salt and pepper. Use as required.

2

2

3

Index